On the Back of a Horse

Harnessing the Healing Power of the Human-Equine Bond

Claire Dorotik, MA

iUniverse, Inc.
Bloomington

The information, ideas, and suggestions in this book are not intended as a substitute
for professional advice. Before following any suggestions contained in this book, you
should consult your personal physician or mental health professional. Neither the
author nor the publisher shall be liable or responsible for any loss or damage allegedly
arising as a consequence of your use or application of any information or suggestions
in this book.

iUniverse books may be ordered through booksellers or by contacting:

iUniverse
1663 Liberty Drive
Bloomington, IN 47403
www.iuniverse.com
1-800-Authors (1-800-288-4677)

Because of the dynamic nature of the Internet, any web addresses or links contained in
this book may have changed since publication and may no longer be valid. The views
expressed in this work are solely those of the author and do not necessarily reflect the
views of the publisher, and the publisher hereby disclaims any responsibility for them.

Any people depicted in stock imagery provided by Thinkstock are models,
and such images are being used for illustrative purposes only.

Certain stock imagery © Thinkstock.

ISBN: 978-1-4502-9008-1 (sc)
ISBN: 978-1-4502-9010-4 (hc)
ISBN: 978-1-4502-9009-8 (ebook)

Printed in the United States of America

iUniverse rev. date: 02/14/2011

Dedication:

To Bill Herring, Sandy Nisson, Kathy Simm, Walt Rutherford, Dr. Reilly, Dr Giovanni Aponte, and all of the horses in my life who provided me with hope and understanding.

Contents

Introduction

People have always been fascinated with horses. From mankind's first experiences with them, either through the parochial methods made timeless by the Spaniards (and later the Spanish riding school), or through the natural horsemanship techniques first mastered by Native Americans, horses have represented a power greater than man. To be sure, horses, for centuries, (and many would argue still today), were associated with wealth, and the pillaging of towns and villages frequently included the theft of many horses. Yet not only have horses represented power and wealth to man, but the mystique of something that is both not entirely understood, and not fully controlled. In considering man's long history with horses, and the endless fascination we have always had with them, it is not hard to see why we would be equally intrigued with the idea that horses can, in some way, help heal what we cannot seem to heal ourselves.

Yet in turning to horses to help us understand ourselves more clearly, we have committed a sinful error. We have done what we do so often with things we do not understand -- we have applied our own understanding to them. In the field of what is now known as equine facilitated psychotherapy, we have failed to account for the very agent of healing, that is, the horse. Traditional methods of equine assisted psychotherapy and learning have looked only at the way the person has responded to the horse, all the while failing to miss the central point of the way in which the *horse* has responded to the person. This fallacy has occurred so much so that the horse has been treated as no more significant than any other non-living therapeutic entity, such as a child's sand tray, or an adult's crossword puzzle. This practice has even gone so far as to ask people to do things with horses that are completely unnatural for them, such as, walking over tarps, painting them, and placing balls on their backs and heads, in the service of "helping people understand themselves better." Practitioners have even offered that it is not the way the horse responds that is of any significance, but rather, they way the patient responds to the horse, thereby completely neglecting the very thing that is purported to be the agent of healing. The consensus of practitioners now also conclusively promulgate the idea that horses "mirror" human emotions, which is a clear example of the need to make horses – that which is not understood – a reflection of ourselves. If a horse is said to "mirror" a human, does this not ignore the very concept that horses themselves have their own emotions? Wouldn't their own emotions express themselves in ways that are unique to horses, and not simply reflections of us? Especially when we are turning to horses to help us "learn about ourselves" why must our need to apply our own understanding of them come before actually learning to understand their language?

As a licensed clinical psychotherapist for more than ten years, but more importantly, a horse trainer for more than twenty years, I decided to write this book to shed insight into an area of the field that I feel has not only been completely overlooked, but sorely misunderstood. It is my belief that in the field of equine facilitated psychotherapy and learning, we have missed the very science that can most help us – that is, the horse's own unique language, and just what *horses* mean through their responses to people. Using narrative examples from my own introduction into the science of horses' language, along with the most current research on equine behavior, it is my hope that, through this book, you, the reader, can come to more fully understand horses' *own* unique language. In comparing the ways in which horses respond to trauma amongst themselves, with the ways in which people manage trauma – again, using examples from my own education on this subject – I hope to clarify just how horses *live* in the unconscious, and the ways in which people *avoid* it – especially in the case of trauma. My intention is to provide a clear premise for why people are so often unaware of themselves, and how through comprehending the language of horses, they can come to understand themselves – and what is unconscious to them – more clearly. In the final chapter, I offer you three case studies, examples of people struggling with their own self-awareness, and the ways in which the horses' responses helped them to recognize repressed emotions, and just how they moved forward where they had been previously stuck. Lastly, it is my most sincere hope that in reading this book you not only come to understand horses more clearly, but also, yourself.

My introduction to what equine facilitated psychotherapy *really* is was one that, like most moments of sagacity, left me utterly speechless. Even of more consequence to me was the fact that I had known horses my entire life, having ridden for almost as many years, and been involved in every aspect of the horse business from training, breeding, showing, transporting and mending horses, from the age of five. Yet I had, as many so often do, failed to consider my horses' capacity for any awareness beyond that of my own. While I recognized horses were highly intuitive and had even had moments with them that evidenced this, I had never once imagined that *they knew more about me, than I knew about me.* In fact, it was the other way around – I thought I knew more about them, than they knew about them.

Yet what I am about to describe, remains, to this day, one of the most profound experiences of my life, and represents the precise moment that shifted my entire perception of what horses are actually capable of thinking, feeling, and knowing about humans.

Chapter One

The Question

J had just returned from what was one of the worst experiences of my life. My father had been violently murdered, and the media had aired and printed photos of his body lying the brush, all over the news, and in the newspaper. As I rushed home from the funeral that day, and slammed the front door behind me, I raced through the living room, desperate to get out to the horses. I couldn't wait to put my riding breeches on, and put the painful memory of the day – my trauma – behind me.

As I walked back through the kitchen, past the family photos that hung on the walls of the old ranch style house that had been our home, and pulled open the sliding glass door to look over toward the arena, the pasture where the mares and foals lived caught my eye. Never before had I paused to watch them, having always been too eager for riding to bother. Yet I stood there, on the porch, my eyes fixed on them, unsure myself even as to why. The three foals, Boomer, Backstreet, and Bien Vida stood together, as they always did, occasionally taking turns to romp through the pasture only to return to the shade of the pepper tree that reached out over the pasture fence.

A movement to my left interrupted my stupor, and my eyes wandered over to Nimo's pen, where he stood looking back my way. His gaze was fixed on me, as if he knew something was different today. Nimo was the three-year-old Oldenburg stallion that I had put off starting all summer. He was the apple of my eye. Born with a confidence and presence uncanny for such a young horse, he was not just breathtaking, but incredibly athletic. So athletic, in fact, that he scared me, at times. The first time I had put him through the jump chute to test his jumping ability, he jumped as high as the 5-foot standards. It wasn't so much that he could jump incredibly well it was that he *knew* he could. He would race down the jump chute, going way too fast, and then just at the right moment – back off, slow down, and explode into the air. After which he would puff himself up, with his typical bravado, as if to say, *Tell me that wasn't the best jump you've ever seen*. He'd hold his head up as high as he could, arching his neck, and snorting ostentatiously. Literally walking on his toes, tail flung up over his back, he looked like a cat trying to be larger than he really was. Nimo had a strut that telegraphed very clearly he had just accomplished something no other horse had.

Taking on everything put in front of him with that kind of confidence was just natural for Nimo. So while he had bravado, sure, it was hardly undeserved. He learned in one lesson, after all, what took the other young horses ten lessons to learn. Yet it was Nimo's interest in people that really separated him from the rest of the horses. Even for a stallion, he was always more interested in me than the others.

One of the 18 horses that were now mine to care for, he was born the year after my mother and I decided to breed our own show jumpers. Curious from the beginning, at only a few days old, he would run up to the fence, away from his mother, as I walked by. I had never had another young horse do that, but then again, when I met Nimo for the first time, at just six hours old, he tried to challenge me. I still remember that day like it was yesterday. As I knelt down in his stall, he came right up, looked at me, paused, and then jumped suddenly, toward me. I jumped back completely surprised, to which he gaily trotted off shaking his head as if to say, *Think twice, ma'am this is my stall*. Who *was* this little horse? I wondered. Six hours old, and he thinks he owns the world. I quickly shooed him away, to let him know that charging people was not acceptable. Surprised as much as I had been, he jumped away. Then, he turned around and came right up to me again. This time, though he seemed to be approaching me out of curiosity. If I was as tough as him, maybe I had something to offer.

Thus began the pattern of our relationship. From that moment on, he was always curious about me, watching as I worked the other horses. Every time I walked by his pen, he'd neigh. Pretty much the next two years of his life seemed to be spent trying to get me to notice him. Of course I loved him, but I had five other riding horses preparing for competitions at the time. Nimo was too young to ride, he just would have to wait. As the months rolled by, I felt as if I was anticipating that first ride as much as he was. But not just with eagerness and excitement – with some fear too.

The determination Nimo showed about everything unsettled me when I thought of starting him under saddle. Independence is a primary characteristic of a stallion, after all, and having me on his back would very likely jeopardize that need. He had always been the master of his world and being ridden would change all that. Moreover, while he wanted my attention, I also knew how much he loved to challenge me. This is what had kept me from starting him.

Standing there, on the front porch now, looking out across the arena, and the pastures stretching out beyond, it occurred to me that I had not spoken to a single person about what had just happened. Nor had I any intention of doing so.

And then it hit me, just as it must have hit Nimo. "*You need to focus here-on me,*" his look seemed to say. Horses were the only thing that hadn't seemed to let me down. And there was an increasingly large part of me that would rather have been one. Nimo knew it, and brought my attention to it. *You've always been here, with us.* It seemed to me as wise a thing to believe as any other at this point, everything in my world having just collapsed.

Or maybe Nimo just knew I was going to ride him today.

I pulled him out of his pen, and brought him over to the grooming area. He was his characteristic macho self, taking his steps with confidence. He knew how magnificent he was. Running the brush down his neck, and over his back, I thought about how he never seemed to question himself, never worried. And it wasn't just because he was a stallion. He'd been this way from the day he was born. He loved life, and acted as if life loved him back. In a way, it *did*. Everybody loved Nimo. Often, when people came to look at the other sale horses, they asked to see Nimo instead. Neighbors and friends – even people who didn't know anything about horses would always ask about him. He just had this magnetic quality. It made me want what he had. And today, as I was grooming him, still shaken, I could have used some of that confidence. I too, wanted life to love me back, and lately it felt as if it had been doing just the opposite.

Due to the fallout of my family's trauma, I was utterly alone, with no idea what *really* caused it, much like I suppose many of us are when unexpected and tragic things happen. While I felt stunned and paralyzed in every other area of my life, the only thing I could seem to be able to focus on was whether or not Nimo would let me ride him. Would he want to share his confidence, or would he be angry with me for wanting him to? Would he become aggressive? Would he buck, or bolt? Any of these responses was possible, and I would be no match for him. I had grown up riding and training horses, had started several horses, and even galloped a number of racehorses, but I had simply never known a horse as athletic as Nimo. Not a *big* horse, he stood at only 16 hands, but he was incredibly balanced in everything he did. I had spent many hours just watching him play; it was captivating how he could move so fast, and change directions so rapidly, never once losing balance. Indeed, his gymnastic abilities made the other horses look like slow moving elephants. There was just no comparison, and he knew it. It's what made him such an incredible horse.

As I slid the saddle onto his back, he reached back to nip at me as he always did. He had worn the saddle many times before in preparation for being ridden, and his attitude was always a bit bothered, as if to say, *Fine I'll wear that silly thing, but it had better be grateful for the ride.* I put the bridle on, and pulled the reins over his head. Then, giving Nimo a pat on the neck, I walked him out of the grooming stall, and into arena.

My better judgment might have told me to lunge him first to get some of his energy out, but today, I didn't care. In a way, I wanted to spit in caution's face. Perhaps that's what I was doing riding a 3-year-old stallion for the first time with no helmet on, and no one around should I have gotten hurt. But I had to know right now, if I could trust him. I had to know if I was really as bad as I *felt*. If Nimo didn't accept me – if Nimo *hurt* me then that would be my answer.

His neck was arched upward, one eye rolling back in my direction. He was puffing himself up, making his small frame huge for me. I put my foot in the stirrup and placed a little weight in it. He immediately tensed a bit, raising his head up even higher – every muscle rigid, as if preparing to take off. He didn't move, though, so I put a little more weight in the stirrup, and lifted myself off the ground. Again, he tensed, keeping his eye fixed on me, but he didn't move. I was now off the ground, halfway on, but without having swung my leg over his back yet – always the telltale moment for a young horse: not only does he see your leg disconcertingly from the eye on the off side, but, there is also a moment where you are unbalanced, and thus, easily dislodged. This is where most riders come off, as the horse bolts upon seeing your leg come over his back, and you are not yet balanced enough to stay with him. There is just no easy way to do this. Try to go too fast, and you will scare the horse; go too slow, and you extend the amount of time during which you're unbalanced. But right now with Nimo, there was none of the usual debate in my mind.

Usually, having done this many times before, I will wait for the horse to tell me when he's ready. Horses have a way of letting you know that you can be on their back. Their eye will soften, the posture will relax, their head will lower. Looking at Nimo's eye, for the first time in my life, I had no idea what was going through a horse's head. Was it because I felt as though I could not be trusted, that I couldn't tell what he was thinking? Or was it he himself just too distant in this moment to be readable. Somehow in that moment – as I perched half on his back, about to give up any chance of jumping safely back to the ground – it didn't matter to me. Nor would I have reacted any differently had his eye clearly signaled anger or fear. Riding Nimo was the biggest challenge in a career of riding horses. I had waited long enough, reverent enough of my own fear. And fear, like caution, had done me no good. So I swung my leg over.

Nimo immediately tensed even more, and looked back at me, both eyes rolled. He could go in any direction – there really is no way to predict, when a horse is so tense. Normally I would have had to remind myself not to tense, too. But not this time. There simply was no energy left for that kind of worry. And I didn't care whether I ended up on his back or in the dirt.

Settling softly now into the saddle and dropping my leg entirely over his side, I slowly searched for the right stirrup. Nimo kept his eye on me, but his head was tilted to the left. Had he seen my right leg come over? I put the reins in my left hand and stroked his neck on the right side with my right. I thought about gently pulling the right rein so he would have to notice my right leg and give me some idea of how he was going to respond. And on any other day, I would have, instead, I gave him a nudge forward with my legs.

His sides were tight with bound energy, and I squeezed harder than I should have. Often, the first steps forward will spook a young horse, too, as they feel the weight of a rider for the first time. Sometimes as they feel this weight, and perceive the rider moving along *with* them, they'll bolt away in fear. I wanted to push past this; I didn't want to take the time to reassure Nimo. I didn't even have both hands on the reins. I just wanted to *trust* him. And, sure enough, those first steps forward were anything but hesitant. He marched forward with the authority of a horse many years older.

Then, all of the sudden, he swung his head around, arched his back, leapt into the air, and landed cantering off – not so much in fear, as what seemed awfully like glee. Nor was I afraid. I just pushed him forward, gripping the reins in one hand, the other still resting on his neck. Instinctively, I lifted myself up off of his back a bit, supporting my weight with my legs. We galloped around the ring with a big bounding stride better suited to a horse twice his size and he played – hopping and leaping, changing leads every three strides. I just let him go. I didn't have the strength to stop him, and somehow, I knew not to. His head wasn't down; he wasn't trying to get me off. I turned him left, and then right, and he changed leads perfectly, as if he'd been doing it his whole life. It really *was* as if Nimo had done this before, as if he already knew what was supposed to happen. I couldn't avoid trusting this animal. He wasn't trying to be independent. He was just trying to take me with him, to a better place. In his way, he was trying to tell me that I was still alive. *You are still here*, he seemed to be saying, *You are alive. Can you feel it?* His play was exhilarating, and jubilant. I didn't have to try hard to stay with him either. He may have been moving fast, but he was definitely trying to stay underneath me. He squealed with delight, like he was truly happy I was finally riding him.

I brought him back to a trot, after of few minutes of this joyful play, and we went all around the ring circling and bending. I wasn't surprised by Nimo's incredible balance, but what was surprising was how *relaxed* he was. The tension I had felt when I first got on by now, was completely gone, and his whole body seemed at ease. He bent both ways smoothly and easily, collecting and extending his stride without hesitation. It was pure satisfaction for both of us.

I pulled Nimo up and ran my hand along his neck, thanking him. I had no words to describe that moment, but he did. As I sat there praising him, he turned to me and nickered. This wasn't the kind of nicker you'd expect from a stallion either. He was nickering affectionately, the way a mare does with her foal, *You're ok, friend. You're ok.*

I burst into tears, unable to hold it in any longer. Everything just hit me in that moment. All the rage I had felt was gone, and there was only sadness. Just sadness. And yet sitting there, I knew for the first time in my life exactly where I was supposed to be. There was no question, no misunderstanding, no mistrust between this horse and me. No need to hide. Safety was right here.

I slid off his back and as I hit the ground, me knees buckled, sending me right down to the ground, beneath Nimo. I just sat there. I didn't want to move. And I couldn't, really. Sitting under a 3 year old stallion is hardly safe under any circumstances, but just then, I didn't care. I didn't feel any fear, and couldn't stop crying in any event. I must have been there for almost an hour, and Nimo just stood over me, nuzzling my hair. I had never seen this side of him.

He was so concerned and caring, I'd had no idea he had that in him. He didn't seem to care about the other horses. It was like he knew he, like all the rest of the horses, depended on me, just like one of their own. And if I weren't ok, they wouldn't be either.

I don't think I had ever felt that cared for in my life. It was as if this was the first moment of clarity in a lifetime of confusion. I had trained and shown all sorts of horses, of course, and the years had taught me a lot about horses, and life; still I had never understood just how profoundly intuitive they were. All this time, I thought they didn't know what I was trying to hide from everybody else. Yet Nimo was trying to tell me he couldn't *not* know.

Chapter Two
Safety Interrupted

"Primarily dissociating", my professor shifted forward in his chair, and rested his elbows on his knees.

I had asked to meet with Dean of my graduate program because I wanted answers. I wanted to know what the greatest effect of trauma is on a person. I wanted to know just what it is about trauma that enables horses to help -- where people can't. "So when you lose track of time, and memory, that is called dissociating?" I asked, looking at the degrees in frames neatly arranged on the wall behind him, and the piled stacks of paper strewn over his desk. Everything about his office seemed so organized except for his desk. The bookcase behind me held one scholarly text after another lined up in what appeared to be alphabetical order. On top of the coffee table between the chair I was sitting in and the wall, sat a lamp, a box of tissue, and a candle. On the wall to my left hung two large nature prints. One was of the Arizona desert, and the other was Everest: a perfect balance.

I hoped somewhere in the mess that collected on top of his desk he would have an answer, "And dissociation happens with trauma?"

"Dissociation is what happens when you are overwhelmed", he scooted his chair forward.

"Does it cause *total* lack of memory?" I asked, sure there was more to the story.

"It can, among other things," he glanced at the stack of papers on his desk.

"Like what?"

"Well, disorientation, feeling numb, disrupted attention and focus, and the feeling of loss of control, are all symptoms of trauma."

"I thought trauma was what we use to describe war veterans."

"It is," he said, sitting back in his chair.

"But what about people who didn't see anybody die? Or who aren't having nightmares or flashbacks, but are still dissociating, and having trouble with memory and orientation?"

"That is what we call complex trauma," he said, as he thumbed through one of the stacks of paper on his desk.

I watched him as he finally pulled the entire stack onto his lap. "What does that mean?" I asked.

He pulled a piece of paper from the middle of the pile. "Look at this," he said, handing it to me.

"What is it?" I asked taking the paper.

"It is a position statement from the APA. Read it."

The APA stood for the American Psychological Association, which regulates the licensure and operation of counselors, psychotherapists, social workers and psychologists. I read through the paragraph underneath the letterhead. It said that children and adults exposed to extreme interpersonal stress consistently demonstrate psychological disturbances that are not captured in the PTSD diagnosis. In a recent field trial, the APA followed 400 treatment seeking individuals and 128 community residents and found that victims of prolonged interpersonal trauma had a high incidence of problems with regulation of affect, memory and attention, self-perception, interpersonal relations, somatization, and systems of meaning. The paper went on further to say that "these findings raise important issues about the categorical versus the dimensional nature of traumatic stress, as well as the issue of comorbidity in PTSD." It also said that, "Future study in this area is necessary and will constitute the inclusion of a provisional diagnosis of disorders of extreme stress, not otherwise specified (desnos)."

I put the paper down. "What does this mean?" I asked.

"For now we are calling it complex trauma." He paused, letting the words sink in. "It means that trauma, like people you know have had, effects a person in more ways than just having flashbacks and nightmares. When you are under extreme stress, you become detached, emotionally. You feel numb. You have trouble remembering things, yes, but you also have trouble remembering yourself, who you are. You may feel differently about people and things in your life."

I looked down at the paper, "Is this what you mean by dissociation?"

He followed my gaze again, "Well, from a psychological perspective, dissociation is a protective activation of altered states of consciousness. It happens when you feel overwhelmed psychologically. After you return to normal, you can have trouble remembering what you dissociated from."

It was beginning to sink in. "So going through something overwhelming, will make a person dissociate from it, and have trouble remembering it."

"Exactly."

"But do people ever regain those memories?"

He placed the stack of papers back on his desk. "They might. Those memories are not gone. What happens when you dissociate is that the memories are encoded in the mind but are not conscious. You have repressed them."

"What happens when you repress them?" I asked, looking at the stack of papers.

"They become encoded differently. Instead of being stored in your conscious awareness, they are stored in your central nervous system. They become 'body memories' that have a physiological encoding."

"So your body remembers, but your brain forgets."

"Yes," he nodded.

I paused, "But how is it possible to store memory in your central nervous system?"

He leaned forward and rested his elbows on his knees again, "Because when you are under intense stress, your body releases neurohormones, such as cortisol, epinephrine, norepinephrine, vasopressin, oxytocin, and endogenous opioids. So, your body is poised to do what you might have wanted to do, should do – to fight. But you were unable to fight because you were overwhelmed psychologically, so you had to dissociate. But that doesn't mean that your neurochemical preparation to defend yourself goes away, instead you just remain dissociated from it."

"So will that make a person feel kind of out of it?" I asked.

"Yes dissociation – the feeling of being kind of disoriented and detached, having trouble remembering certain events, is a common effect of persistent, overwhelming stress. Desensitization in this way is a form of protection."

"Desensitization to the stress hormones?"

"No, those will still be there. But you will feel detached from yourself, from those around you, from the things in your life that you enjoy," he said, sitting back again.

"Well what happens to the stress hormones? Do they go away?" I asked.

He paused before he said, "No, they remain at high levels."

"Is that bad?" I asked, curious as to the long term effects of elevated neurochemicals.

He looked as if he was searching for a delicate way to phrase things. "It can interfere with your ability to function."

I leaned forward, "How?"

"Well being under extreme stress, your brain begins to change," he said, as he pulled the stack of papers from his desk and began thumbing through them again.

He pulled one out and handed it to me, "Here, look at this."

I took the paper and read it over. It was an abstract from a research study about the long-term effects of extreme stress. The study had found that under severe and chronic stress, changes occur in both the neural pathways of the brain, and the functioning of the hippocampus and the amygdala. "What does this mean?" I asked.

"Well, extreme stress affects the way the brain functions, stores memory, and reacts to things in the environment," he said placing the stack of papers back on the desk.

I looked back the paper. It said that people who had undergone chronic stress had an increased startle response, difficulty differentiating threatening from non-threatening environmental stimuli, and the propensity to return to clinical levels of stress under psychological arousal. "So it's like feeling panicked all the time?" I asked.

"Maybe not all of the time, but feeling reactive to stressful things in the environment." He held his hands out indicating a distance about two feet apart. "See, if this is the spectrum at which, under normal conditions, people can operate, and any amount of stress could be handled within this spectrum, with complex trauma, it is going to be a bit smaller." He moved his hands closer together. "What might not have been troubling before, might now cause panic. The coping range is much smaller." He lowered his hands and rested them on his lap.

I looked at the degrees on the wall behind him. "Does it interfere with the ability to function?" I asked.

"That depends on the person. Certainly people can function for many years under these conditions, but they may find alternative ways of coping."

"Like what?"

He shifted in his chair and crossed his legs. "Many turn to drugs, some isolate or develop habitual patterns to avoid dealing with stressful situations or relationships."

"So how do they get back to normal?" I asked glancing back at the paper.

"It's hard. The goal is to return the CNS back to pre-trauma levels."

"How?"

"Sometimes systematic desensitization can help, sometimes medication, but so far, nothing has been especially effective," he said looking toward the stacks of paper piled on his desk.

"Well, can other people tell when someone experiencing all of these things?" I asked, wondering if people themselves often recognize that they may be dissociating.

"No these things often go undetected by others. Many people can hide them."

In studying the recent research on trauma, I found that what my professor was saying was not news to those who study trauma. While there is no current diagnostic category for complex trauma, medical and behavioral health professionals have had no choice but to use multiple diagnostic categories in an attempt to convey the vast array of difficulties that can be experienced by those who experience prolonged and overwhelming conditions. However, as the name implies, complex trauma involves complex interactions between multiple bio-psycho-social systems. The nervous system becomes stuck in a chronic state of over-activation, causing exaggerated reactions to seemingly harmless stimuli, which then leads to problems with memory, identity, and emotional regulation.

Compounding the problem is the fact that for those with complex trauma, these nervous system effects can have lasting consequences. Many studies have used MRI brain imaging of combat veterans to show reductions in the volume of the right hippocampus, the part of the brain that handles long term memory and navigation, that then become *permanent*. Further studies also found that high levels of glucocorticoids (cortisol in the human) released during stress were associated with damage to neurons in the hippocampus, which indicated lack of growth, a predisposition to stress and disruptions in cellular metabolism. The majority of research also found that stress results in deficits in *new learning* that are in addition to damage in the hippocampus.

Essentially, when trauma happens, the brain is over stimulated with excitatory responses, and not able to regulate them. Like a kid who cannot focus, exposure to stress further reduces the brain's capacity to learn. But this also reduces the capacity to recover as recovery depends on *learning a new normal*. As memory impairment and lapses in judgment lead to changes in internal beliefs, the traumatized person begins to think differently about herself, the world and the future.

And for all of it's recognized effects, still today, complex trauma is referred to by many as the "invisible epidemic" affecting as many

16% of the population. And that is just those who seek treatment. Often, sufferers of psychological trauma may either not recognize their symptoms, or they simply go unnoticed by those around them.

Yet thinking back to my ride on Nimo, it was clear that the symptoms of trauma, do not go unnoticed by horses.

Chapter Three

Among The Herd

The question of whether horses themselves can dissociate had been burning in my mind ever since that day in my professor's office, and as I watched Bill step back and light another cigarette, I pondered how to pose the question without sounding confused.

"Give him a minute," he said, flicking the ashes in the sand.

I reached down and gave Flying Cat a pat on the neck. He caught his breath stretching his neck down as I released the reins. I turned and looked over at the gymnastic we had just jumped through. It was the biggest we had ever jumped. Bill, my coach, had been slowly raising the jumps and making them wider with each time through. Then he would make us wait. He insisted that horses need "time to think." He'd watch Cat closely, and after adjusting the jumps, send us through the gymnastic again.

I never questioned Bill, and when he said it was time to go, I knew Cat was ready. Sixty seven years old, about 5'11' and of a slight build, Bill had accomplished more in his lifetime than most trainers can ever hope to. It was not hard to notice the way people in the horse business regarded him – with a sense of awe. Yet, having trained horses his whole life, he never went anywhere without a healthy dose of humility, a straw hat, and cigarette. Forever the storyteller, he loved to recount how he got into show jumping in the first place. He had started out training reining horses, the kind that run, spin and slide. Yet, over time, his reputation for being able to work with any horse spread. He could turn an obstreperous rogue into a polished show horse. Yet when a customer brought over a rangy looking Thoroughbred, Bill promptly told him that Thoroughbreds are not reining horses. They are not built for the fast spins and slides like Quarter horses. They're too tall and their center of gravity is too high. But the customer pleaded. Every trainer around had rejected the horse and Bill was his last stop. Bill took a look at the horse, a tall, bay gelding. The customer told him that he had bucked off every other trainer and he didn't know what to do with him. "What does he like to do?" Bill asked.

"Well he seems to like jumping out of his pen. I can't keep him anywhere," he answered.

A little smile came across Bill's lips as he told the story. He always liked a rogue.

Well what became of that rogue is recorded in Olympic history. His name was Fleet Apple. He was on the 1968 US Olympic Show Jumping team. And he never did learn how to turn. When the chef d'equip of the team called Bill to tell him that they couldn't turn the horse, Bill chuckled. "He turns off the leg. If you use the rein, he locks his jaw. It's an old reining trick." There was a pause on the line, "Oh, oh, okay. We'll try that." Bill could tell the team captain had never heard of such a thing.

Being innovative in his training methods was only one thing Bill was known for. It was due largely to his efforts that grand prix competition was brought to California. Previous to that, grand prix events only existed on the east coast. There wasn't even an organization for horse show competition until Bill and many others began advocating for one. What started as a group of trainers, judges, and riders became known as the Pacific Coast Horseman's Association, now one of the largest equestrian organizations in the nation.

I had begun working with Bill three years before, when a horse show judge suggested that he could help with my "rogue" thoroughbred, Keeper. From the time I started with him, Bill's knowledge of horses amazed me. He literally thought like a horse.

I walked Cat a little closer to where he was standing, resting one arm on the jump standard. "Hey Bill, do you think horses can tell if people are dissociating?" I asked.

He looked at me quizzically. "If they're what?"

"You know – like, not there emotionally."

"Well they're herd animals." He looked at me as if this, in itself, answered the question.

"What does that mean?" I had never before thought about what it would mean to be a herd animal.

"That's how they look at people, too, like part of the herd."

"How would that make them able to tell what going on with people emotionally?" I still didn't understand this.

"Because that's how a herd relates-all on the same emotional level. If one horse gets upset, they all get upset. If one gets nervous, they all get nervous." He pulled his arm off of the standard, and walked toward the edge of the ring. He returned with a small branch he had picked up off the ground, "Let me show you something." He took out his cigarette lighter and lit the branch. It immediately began to burn, creating a bright orange flame and a plume of smoke. Cat started to back up. His eyes went wide as he caught sight of the flame. He snorted, turning his head side to side to get another look at it. Bill just stood still holding the simmering branch in front of him as Cat continued backing up nervously. He had gone from resting quietly to a palpable panic.

"Hear that?" he asked.

I turned my head toward the barn hidden behind the house. Keeper, my rogue thoroughbred, was neighing nervously. I listened again. Another neigh. It sounded like Sylvie, one of the mares in the pasture on the other side of the house. Then another, and another. Soon, a chorus of neighs surrounded us.

I looked at Bill, standing there still holding the branch, with a grin on his face. "Now how did those other horses know Cat was nervous?" he asked.

The barn and the pasture were both at least 400 meters from the arena, too far out of earshot to hear the small crackling of the branch, or even the snort Cat let out. Nor could the small amount of smoke generated by the flame be detected at that distance. "I have no idea. How did they?"

"They feel it. Because they are all on the same emotional wavelength, when one member gets nervous, it affects the emotional flow of the herd."

I had read that certain animals, like birds or fish, could communicate like this. Without actually seeing the leader of a flock, an individual bird could sense the directional changes of the flock. Another study found that schools of fish when placed in adjacent tanks, separated by a barrier entirely blocking their sight, continued to swim in the same direction, as if there were no barrier. Even though they could no longer see the other fish, or sense the current changes created by the swimming pattern, they continued to swim in the same direction.

But these were directional changes. What had just happened here involved an emotional connection between all of the horses; without being able to see, hear, or smell any trace of Cat's panic, the other horses had nonetheless felt it. "It's like a sixth sense," I said, looking at Cat as he watched Bill put out the branch.

"Sort of, yeah."

I thought back to the conversation in my professor's office. "So horses don't repress their emotions?" I asked

He looked at me quizzically again, "They don't what?"

"They don't push their emotions away. You know, like try to not feel them."

"They can't. See all of those horses that were just neighing, they didn't know why they were neighing. It was just instinctual. They knew something was wrong. It's how they keep themselves safe."

So if Cat actually had been in danger, the herd would have known about it and responded, I thought to myself. It made so much sense. That's why horses don't hide their emotions, because the herd will always respond to them. Even if they don't know *why* something is wrong, they will respond anyway. So there is never a *need* to hide their emotions.

I flipped back to that day I decided to ride Nimo for the first time. I could see him standing in his pen, staring at me intently. I wondered what he seemed to notice that I didn't.

"So what do they do when people hide their emotions?" I asked.

"They can't." Bill pulled out another cigarette and lit it.

"What do you mean?" I wondered if he was referring to horses or people.

He put the cigarettes back in his pocket. "Horse's can't avoid responding to people's emotions. Even if you try to hide them, to the horses, they are still there."

"They respond to them, even if you think you have hidden them." I reached down and scratched Cat's neck. He was still looking suspiciously at the extinguished branch on the ground.

Bill nodded.

"What if you don't know that you have hidden them?" I wondered about the complex trauma that my professor was talking about. Those people don't even know they have repressed their feelings.

"To the horses, they are still there."

So because horses' entire communication system is built around responding to each other's emotions, they *can't* repress them. Unlike people, they have to respond to them. It is part of their instinctual nature.

I had experienced exactly what this meant while training horses -- that when they become overwhelmed with fear, they can't stop it and will sometimes run right through a fence blinded by fear. In fact, the whole concept of "sacking out" a horse is based on the idea that if you can overcome a horse's fear response -- essentially his instinct to run -- by repeatedly desensitizing him to a scary object, like a plastic bag, then he will no longer respond to fearful objects by running. However, sacking out doesn't always work. A friend of mine tried a form of sacking out with her mare by tying a plastic bag on to the horse's saddle and then turning her loose in a pen. Her horse, in a full-blown state of terror, ran right through the fence, out of the pen, and through a series of three more fences, severely cutting her legs, chest and shoulders. Her "fight-or-flight response", had simply taken over, and she was unable to stop. Because of horses' prey design, this extreme instinct for flight or fight is their hard-wired physiology, they cannot consciously override it like people can -- it is what has kept them as a species alive for so long. When frightened they have to move their feet, and often restricting this response to run, will increase it.

But it seems that the response to run does more for the horse than simply evade prey. Several studies have demonstrated that horse's flight response actually results in a surge of dopamine, a powerful opium-like neurotransmitter, in the brain. After running from a threatening object, dopamine then helps the horse essentially calm back down. This effect is adaptive in that it prepares the horse to run from future threats. While the horse can't stop himself from running from a perceived threat, fleeing itself, is a way to self-adjust the physiological responses, and restore a state of physiological calm.

But expressing their emotions -- and thereby responding to their fear, and not restricting their need to run -- is also a way for the herd to connect together physiologically. Once one horse feels something, the entire herd feels it too -- it's the only communication system they know.

Yet I had also seen horses communicate with people this way. As a competitive rider, I had once seen the same horse be perfectly well behaved for child rider, yet act out, violently, when ridden by the child's trainer. While at first this seemed antithetical to what would be expected as the child's riding ability was not nearly as developed as that of the trainer. Yet in watching how both the child and the trainer interacted with other people, the answer was obvious. While the little kid was friendly, sweet, playful, and perhaps a bit timid, the middle-aged trainer was short with others, inpatient, and even verbally abusive toward his students. Essentially, the trainer was in flight response all of the time, yet he wasn't running anywhere -- therefore, he wasn't responding, really, to his flight response. To the horse, acting out was the only way to attempt to get the trainer to pay attention to what was happening inside him, and in doing so, respond to his own physiological need. Instead of repressing this physiology, the horse was trying to bring it to the surface for the trainer. It was as if the horse's behavior was saying to the trainer, 'you have intense anger in you that needs to come out'.

So when people don't know that they have repressed their emotions, or even what those emotions are, the horses do. It all made so much sense.

Chapter Four

Disordered Attachment

"Okay, speeding up," Dr. Reilly punched a key on her computer.

The faces flashed a little faster: smiling face, a frowning face, a grimacing face. I pushed the buttons on the keyboard, one for happy, two for sad, three for afraid, and four for angry. The faces kept flashing on the computer screen.

"That's a one second interval," she said, punching another key.

I pushed the two key as the sad face flashed again. The grimacing face flashed. I pushed the four key. The happy face flashed and I hit the two key, "Oops," I said out loud.

"It happens. Here's .5 seconds." She clicked the key on her computer again.

The faces went faster now. I struggled to keep up: one, four, two, one, three. "Damn," I whispered. It was getting harder.

"Last one, .25 seconds. This is the time we get in most social interactions." She pushed the key again.

I watched the faces on the screen. They were flashing so fast it was like a blur. My fingers fumbled the keys. "Man, how does anyone keep up?" I asked, staring at the screen.

"Amazing eh?" She pushed her chair back from her desk and turned toward me.

"Are you serious? That is really the speed of most social interactions?" I rotated my chair to face her.

"Yep."

I had come to the research lab at San Diego State University on the advice of the American Psychological Association (APA). I contacted them because I wanted to know if people can function when they avoid their emotions. After being shown their position statement about complex trauma, I figured they might know where to find my answer. They had directed me to Dr. Reilly. Without hesitation they told me that if anyone knows just how avoiding emotions affects a person, it would be her.

Dr. Reilly had been studying emotions since the beginning. As a graduate student, she became interested in the way people process emotions. Convinced that not all people can read emotions in the same way, she began searching for a way to test this. However, testing whether or not people can read emotions is difficult.

She had begun with interviews, lots of interviews. Enticing undergraduates, friends, relatives, neighbors, anyone she could think of to participate in a one-on one conversation with another person, she compiled a massive amount of research. The first person, the speaker, was to speak about a given topic, such as a fond memory, a first pet, a family vacation, or a horrible tragedy, for one minute, while the second person, the listener, was asked to then record the speaker's mood at four intervals: 15 seconds, 30 seconds, 45 seconds, and 60 seconds. These results were then compared to the speaker's recollection of her mood at these intervals, when watching herself on the videotape replay of the interview.

The problem was that both participants got it wrong. When Dr. Reilly paused the videotape on a single frame, and correlated that to the time intervals, the facial expression didn't match either person's recollection of the emotion conveyed on the speaker's face. While she suspected the listener would misread the emotion conveyed by the speaker's face, she had never anticipated that the speaker would misread *her own* emotions. Consistently speakers would say they were happy, when a video frame of their face clearly showed a grimace. Or they would say they were afraid, while the still frame clearly revealed a smile. However, if Dr. Reilly moved the tape to the next frame forward, or the previous frame, the speaker's recollections sometimes were correct. As the time interval between frames shortened, the participant's error rates went up. Yet with greater time windows, a wider range of expression would be expressed, and therefore the participant's recollected emotion would more often be captured in the time interval. What this meant was that as the tape played at a faster speed, the facial expressions would appear to be consistent with the speaker's recollections. Yet when Dr. Reilly slowed the tape, something strange happened. The facial expression would change, instantaneously, from one emotion to another, and then back again. A person's facial expression would look happy in one frame, and then grimace in the next, and then return to happy again in the next. It wasn't until Dr. Reilly slowed the time interval down to .25 seconds that she realized this. The speed of emotional expression was too fast for the participants to predict.

This result fascinated Dr. Reilly, but also left her with no answers. Still, some participants appeared to be more accurate at predicting both their own emotions, and those of others. She wanted to know why.

She had, however, isolated the time interval at which facial expressions change: .25 seconds. In order to determine why made some people were better at reading emotions than others, she would need to use a test method at this speed that would hold constant. She'd have to use the actual videotape of the speaker, and not the real speaker. This way, she could be sure of the emotion expressed on the face she was looking at.

The faces on the computer I had just been watching were the result of thousands of hours of videotape. The frames had been lifted from the tape and scanned into the computer to allow for variation in speed, but to also make sure the faces the study subjects saw would not be from the same person. The happy face might be from a young girl in one frame, and from an older man the next. Dr. Reilly wanted to make sure that she was testing people's ability to read *all* emotional expression, not just the expression from one subject. She was worried that the reason some people could read emotions better was because they could read emotions better on *specific* people. If one of the participants happened to be attempting to read the emotions of the other participant, a young girl, for example, was it that the face she saw was that of a young girl that made the difference, or was it something else that made this person better at reading emotions? The only way Dr. Reilly could know was to use a variety of faces.

I looked across at the row of computers to my left. There were five of them. I glanced behind me, six more computers. This allowed Dr. Reilly to test twelve people at once. The test only took five minutes. I wondered how many people she had tested. "Does anyone get it right?" I asked.

She took her glasses off and set them on her desk. "It's very rare. We don't see it much."

"What does it take?"

"What does it take to be able to read emotions correctly?" she asked, glancing back at her computer screen.

"Yeah, I mean, why can some people do it, and others can't?"

"I'll show you. Watch this." She pointed to her screen.

It was a videotape of a small room that was completely bare except for a few small stuffed animals in the corner. Then the room's only door opened and a woman holding a baby walked in. The child appeared to be between one and two years. Setting her down in the middle of the room, the woman turned and promptly exited the room. The child immediately began to cry. Then a different woman entered the room, picked up one of the small stuffed animals and sat next to the child. Using the stuffed animal, she attempted to console her. She made smiley faces and wiggled the animal in front of the child, but the young girl was inconsolable. Despite what the woman did, she continued to cry, and kept her eyes fixed on the door. After a minute, the child's mother returned. She immediately went to the teary youngster and picked her up. Hugging her and gently bouncing her up and down, she attempted to console her. The mother kept hugging and bouncing. The child kept crying. The more the mother attempted to soothe her, the more the child clung to her.

The screen went black. "What was that?" I asked, looking at Dr. Reilly.

It is called the strange situation. It is a test, developed by a researcher, Dr. Mary Ainsworth, to determine a child's attachment style."

"Attachment style?"

"Attachment style describes the way people learn to have relationships. It's the way that they become close to others."

"Isn't closeness something we all do the same way?"

A small grin came across her face, "Here, watch this." She pushed a key on her computer. The screen opened again to the same small room, with the same stuffed animals in the corner. A different woman walked in, again, holding a baby. The baby appeared to be the same age as the first. Again, the woman put the child in the center of the room and promptly left. He immediately began to cry. Then the same woman from the first tape entered the room, and again attempted to console him. She sat next to the child and jiggled the animal in front of him, yet he kept his eyes on the door, and continued crying. The woman kept waving the toy in front of the youngster and smiling. Then the child paused, and looked at the toy. He looked at the woman, and then back at the door. The woman kept smiling and moving the toy. Watching the toy, the child stopped crying. He looked at the woman's face and giggled. He reached for the toy, and giggled more. Then the door opened and the mother returned. She immediately went to the baby, picked him up, and hugged and bounced him. The child giggled and hugged back.

Dr. Reilly pushed a key on her computer and the screen went black again. "See the difference?" she asked.

"Yeah. So why did one baby keep crying, and the other stopped?"

"It has to do with the way they attach to their mothers. The first one is what we call anxious attachment. It means that the child cannot be calmed by a stranger when the mother leaves, and clings to her when she returns. Basically, the child is anxious about the mother leaving, and cannot be soothed."

"What about the second one?" I asked.

"Well the second one is what we call secure attachment. Here the child worries at first when the mother leaves but can be soothed by a stranger, and is comforted when the mother returns. The child feels safe enough about the mother, and people in general, to be soothed by a stranger, and also comforted when the mother returns. She doesn't worry about the mother like the first."

"So the first one is worried about being close with her mother and others, and the second one feels secure about being close."

"Yes."

I looked back at the screen, "But what does this have to do with avoiding emotions?"

"Well, the first one avoids emotions because she is too worried to read them correctly," she said, glancing at the screen, "and people with that attachment style do very poorly on the test you just took."

"You mean the first baby was too worried to correctly read her mother's soothing?" I asked.

"Exactly. You noticed that she was not calmed by the stranger, or her mother. She was fixated on being worried about her mother. She was not able to read any other emotion but that."

"She just kept crying no matter what."

"Right, that became the dominant emotion, blocking any others," she said, putting her glasses back on.

"So in a way she avoids any emotion but being worried," I glanced back at the rows of computers, "and if she were to take the test as an adult, you would notice a difference between her and the second one."

"Right."

"And the second one could be worried, but then be calmed down too. So she doesn't avoid emotions?" I asked.

"Right."

"But these are just babies, I mean won't the first one eventually stop worrying?"

Dr. Reilly looked right at me, "No, attachment styles don't change. They are constant over the course of a person's life."

I looked over at the computer I had been tested on, "You mean the anxious baby will always be too worried to read emotions correctly?"

"Yes, and she will also worry that other's will leave her. Her worry about them will get in the way of healthy relationships. She will not be able to differentiate her needs from those of others."

"Differentiate her needs?"

"She will be too bound by worry about others to figure out what she needs."

I thought back to some of the people that had come for equine therapy sessions. While more often than not, people new to horses had wanted to be close to the horse, there were some that had seemed to insist on being dangerously close. They too, couldn't read the expression, or even the behavior, of the horse enough to realize when they could potentially get stepped on. Even when I had pointed out the danger, and suggested, "protecting themselves," they'd find themselves back in the same position. As if they had a need to be close that overrode even the need to be safe, these were the people I'd worried about the most. I'd find myself constantly watching over them, and my own anxiety raised, as I contemplated how to allow them an interaction with the horse that would not result in an injury. But, interestingly, the horses hadn't shared my anxiety about these people. Instead, they pushed back at them. Even horses that were normally aloof would nudge, shove, and move into the space of the people who wanted to be too close. And they would continue, persistently, as if trying to provoke a reaction from them. I had always explained this as a herd animal's way of engaging a needed response from a person. Because the person who wants to be too close, and puts herself in danger is not effectively, a good herd member, the horse works to make her do what she needs to do to be a better herd member. The way the horses see it, when the person predisposes herself to danger, she also predisposes the entire herd to danger -- as the herd then has to protect and watch out for her -- and the horse, through his pushy behavior, attempts to force her to correct this by learning to first protect herself. If she can learn to keep herself safe with the horse, a fellow herd member, then she can also learn to be safe against other predators.

But a part of me had also assumed that those that wanted to be too close were just not "horse people" and lacked the savvy that comes with years of working with large animals. Yet considering the exaggerated reactions of the horses, it was clear there was something much deeper that propelled their behavior. Perhaps it wasn't just that they couldn't read the emotions of the horse, but rather, that they couldn't read *any* emotions very well. I turned back toward Dr. Reilly, "So because of the way you learn to attach to your mother, you can either read emotions correctly or not?"

She paused, considering her answer, "Well for the most part yes. There are other types of attachment styles though. There's the two you saw, anxious and secure. And then there is avoidant and disorganized."

"Avoidant and disorganized don't sound like they read emotions correctly either." I said, still contemplating what this all meant.

"No they don't. The only one that does is the secure style."

I thought back to the equine sessions, "But wait, how can you test that now?"

"You mean with adults?" she asked.

"Yes."

"Well we use what is called an attachment styles inventory. It's a questionnaire that determines your attachment style."

"And it's accurate?"

She looked right at me again, "Very."

"But how do you know for sure?" I asked.

"Because it is correlated with longitudinal studies that follow people over the course of their lifetime, beginning from birth. What these studies show is that not only do the types of relationships these people have not change, but their results on the test don't change either."

"So what is the percentage of people who can read emotions correctly?" I asked looking over at the twelve computers lined against the walls of the room.

"About eight percent."

"Only eight percent?" I looked back at her.

"Yes." She said as she reached up and turned her computer off.

"Why so few?"

"Attachment styles don't change, so if you developed an anxious style as a child, this will affect the way you raise your own children. Anxious mother's tend to have anxious babies, and avoidant mothers tend to have avoidant babies."

"So only eight percent of the population tends to read emotions correctly?" I asked.

She looked past me at the small section of the lab that held the computers, "That's under the best circumstances, here in the lab, with no distractions. Outside of here, when we are distracted, that number may be even less."

"So does that mean that less than eight percent of the population can have healthy relationships too?"

"Not necessarily. People can learn to function, but reading emotions is a different business."

"You mean that they can function reasonably well, but they won't really know what is going on with themselves, and others emotionally."

"Precisely," she said.

I wondered if that was functioning at all.

Chapter Five

How It Begins

"Watch your left rein," Kathy called from the end of the arena.

I pulled General up and gave him a pat, "Did I catch him again?"

"He's a little *here*," she brought her arms toward her front, pointing them down and to the left. "Come through again."

I picked up the reins, and looked down making sure they were even this time. Giving General a nudge, we headed down through the gymnastic. He eagerly moved off energetically like a rubber ball bounced off a concrete floor -- making it challenging to keep him straight. Three four foot effortless bounds later, we landed easily and cantered off. Pulling him up, I turned toward Kathy.

"Perfect," she said, walking toward us. "He was absolutely square in front." She brought her arms in front, bent at the elbow and pointing her hands straight down toward the ground, symbolized General's correct form.

Kathy had been nagging me about my left rein ever since I started working with her. Apparently I rode crooked, with a shorter left rein. I'd had no idea until she pointed it out – all of the horses jumped with their legs pointed slightly to the left. I would've never noticed, it felt normal to me. I know I rode with more weight in my right stirrup – I had started doing that after breaking my left foot at sixteen. One of my mother's horses had slipped in the wet footing and fallen, crushing it sideways. I guess I now compensated by holding the left rein tighter than the right.

A persistent coach, Kathy was determined that she was going to fix it. She had come into my life sometime in the middle of my career as a jumper rider, and toward the end of hers. In my desperation to sell horses, I had left messages with almost every trainer I could think of, whether I knew them or not, yet surprisingly, it was Kathy who had left a message for me.

I had never met her before, and only seen her at horse shows -- mostly in the judge's box. I had ridden in her classes many times, and she always placed me well. But I really had no idea she knew who I was.

When I picked up the phone to call her back, she said that she had always admired my riding, and would like the opportunity to work with me. She also said she had a horse she thought I could help.

That began our relationship. She would coach me on my horses in exchange for my help fixing her horse, General. And although she proved to be an absolute perfectionist, everything she did was in kindness. Never a correction without a compliment first, her tutelage was patient but firm – it was what she known for. Considered by everybody in the horse show world as the expert on young horses, she specialized in developing them from babies, to horse show champions. She could take a nervous youngster and turn him into a calm, confident competitor.

But when she met General, he was a bit too boisterous for her. A riding accident years before had caused her to be more careful. She had been standing at in gate at the Los Angeles Equestrian Center, waiting for her turn to ride the grand prix course, when something spooked her horse and he reared up falling over backwards, landing on top of her. She was knocked out cold, her head suffering a massive pounding that resulted in a coma that lasted eight days. The doctors didn't know what to expect, but remained doubtful as to any chance she may have to regain consciousness without serious loss of function. When she finally did wake up a week and a day later, life looked a little different. She no longer took it for granted. Amazingly, the only impairment she suffered was a loss of equilibrium. But the experience taught her that life, all life was precious.

I dropped the reins and scratched General's neck. He saw Kathy walking toward us and started toward her. "Better that time?" I asked.

"Did you notice the difference?"

"Yeah, he was even *more* like riding a bouncing ball," I answered giving him a pat.

She laughed as General placed his head against her chest. She reached up and scratched behind his ears, "Are you a bouncing ball General?"

A movement to my left caught my eye, "Gotta another one there, huh?" I asked.

She turned to see her young foals playing in the pasture next to the arena. Russell, one of the babies was hopping and leaping in circles around Sunday, the other baby. The mares, Chloe and Holly, were casually munching hay nearby. "Looks like it, doesn't it?"

"He's the more energetic of the two?" I asked.

"Well all of Chloe's babies are. They are just on the muscle all the time. Liza's that way."

Liza was Chloe's three-year old daughter that I had been riding for the last two months. Kathy had told me upon starting that I'd never get to the bottom of her. I didn't know what that meant, and only found out when Liza would come back from a ride fully covered in sweat and still full of it. I had been trying to get her to relax and stay calm when ridden, but no matter what I did, she wouldn't. Our first rides were over an hour long. I kept reassuring her, and reaching down to pet her as we went, but she refused to relax, insisted on going fast. Everywhere we went it had to be fast. I didn't want to constantly pull on the reins to slow her down, and was determined to teach her to relax on her own. But after two weeks of this, Kathy reminded me again that I would never get to the bottom of her. She was just an energetic and tense horse. "What about Holly's babies, are they that way too?" I asked.

"Well, take a look," she answered looking down at the pasture.

Sunday, Holly's foal was calmly munching hay as Russell was running by, nipping at her sides, trying to get her to play.

"They couldn't care less. Nothing riles Holly's babies. *She* was that way, that's what made her such a great show horse."

I reached down to loosen the girth and let General relax, "Kathy, do you think that being energetic and tense gets in the way of horses making attachments?"

She looked up at me surprised, "What do you mean?"

"Well do you think that because Russell and Liza are tense horses, that they have trouble becoming close to other horses?"

"No, it's the opposite," she said.

"You mean that because they are tense, they have an easier time becoming close, and attaching to other horses?"

"Well, they have to."

"Why?"

"Here, I'll show you," she said as she turned to walk toward the pasture. Beto, her groom, was walking down the hill from the barn. Kathy called to him as she approached the mares and babies. Heading over, Kathy handed him a halter, and they entered the pasture together. Kathy put the halter on Russell, and Beto haltered Sunday. Together they led them out of the pasture. The mares both stopped eating and came over, curious as to what was going on. Chloe was in front, attempting to follow Russell. Holly was concerned as well, watching as Kathy and Beto led the babies away from them and across the ranch. Chloe started calling and galloping along the fence as she watched Russell being escorted away. He called back nervously. Kathy kept him moving forward, but he repeatedly turned back and called to his worried mother. Sunday was less concerned, and had found the pocket full of carrots that Beto always kept. Her nose plastered on his back pocket, she was determined to dodge Beto's attempts to fend her off.

Finally, Beto and Kathy reached a paddock about 200 meters from the mares. Small and square, it shared a fence with the pasture that held the retired horses. As Kathy and Beto entered with the babies, probably twenty of them, all different ages, came running over.

Kathy had also developed a reputation as a specialist in rehabilitating injured horses. Some of them were in the middle of their show careers and would hopefully return to work. Others were past their prime and we enjoying the last years of their life. Then there were a few young ones who would never work. These were the ones who had been injured before they ever started. For them, life would be spent in the herd, not the show ring.

Kathy and Beto took the halters off. Sunday immediately ran over to the fence, curious about the new herd of horses. Russell turned back and ran to the fence closest to Chloe, nervously calling. The herd called back. Sunday had already reached the fence, but they were not interested in her. Attempting to get their attention, she reached over the fence and nuzzled at them, but they kept their eyes fixed on Russell. One of them pushed her nose out of the way, nearly knocking her over, as he paced up and down the fence, calling to Russell. Russell heard the commotion behind him and turned to look, then turned toward Chloe, and then again toward the herd. He took a few steps toward them. Pausing, he looked back at Chloe. She was racing around wildly, and calling. He took a few more steps toward the herd, and looked back at Chloe again. Finally, he trotted toward the herd. They immediately gathered around the fence greeting him. Sunday came running over and they pushed her out of the way, and pushed each other out of the way to get to Russell. As they reached to nuzzle him, he gaped his mouth open and closed several times indicating submissiveness. They nuzzled him persistently. He continued to be submissive. They kept nuzzling. Finally, he started to calm down, stopped gaping his mouth and nuzzled back. Pushing his entire body against the fence, he leaned into it and the herd all put their noses on him. Chloe continued to call, but Russell had stopped. The herd had calmed him.

Kathy started back toward the arena. General watched as she made her way up the small hill from the pasture, and entered the ring, pausing to glance back toward the paddock. Russell was still huddled against the fence, the herd nuzzling him. Sunday had given up and was munching hay again.

"Why are they so interested in Russell?" I asked.

"Because he needs it more," she said, scratching General's forehead.

"But he is the one who wasn't interested in them at first," I said looking over at Sunday.

"That's right."

"But I don't understand, why would that make them more interested in him?"

She turned to look back at Russell, "Because he was also too nervous to trust them at first."

"So that made them more interested in him?" I asked, watching the herd as they remained huddled around Russell, like football players around a quarterback.

"Yes."

"But why?"

"Because it is *unsafe*."

"What is unsafe?"

"Not trusting."

I looked down at General as he planted his head against Kathy's chest. It's true that to horses, there exists no relationship without trust. Having worked with many horses that had been abused, and had their trust broken, I had witnessed just how differently the herd responds when trust has been broken. My horses would *always* take more interest in whatever new injured horse was brought in, surrounding him while gently sniffing all over his body. Several observational studies have also demonstrated that the frequency of affectionate behaviors (sniffing, rubbing, and nuzzling) are greater when injured horses are introduced into a herd than when non-injured horses are introduced. However, I had also seen horses become more interested in people for similar reasons. A good friend of mine, Casey, accompanied me to the barn one day, as she had many times before, and upon asking to spend some time with my horse Nimo, I put him in the round pen loose with her. While in the past, Nimo had always been affectionate with myself and everyone else, what I saw with Casey that day was clearly a deviation from his normal behavior. He was incessant in his approach and circled around Casey repeatedly, holding his body very close to hers, despite the fact that she became a bit nervous about this. As he came closer and closer to Casey, she slowly backed toward the fence, and he appeared to be pushing her there. Eventually, with her back to the fence, Nimo held Casey still, curving his body around her, essentially preventing any escape or movement. Yet there was no expression of anger, and Nimo's behavior didn't appear to be done in dominance. Casey had also spent time with many of my horses before, and had developed a sense of ease around them, but they not had responded to her in the same way as currently Nimo was. When I later asked her if anything was different that day, she revealed that she had lost her job, and having no money in savings, was incredibly frightened about her future. Despite the fact that I had known her for many years, I wouldn't have noticed that anything was different without witnessing Nimo's behavior. Once we began to talk about Casey's plight, it became obvious to both her and I that her fear was, in fact, panic.

Even though what I saw between Casey and Nimo did involve affection, Nimo was actually moving Casey from one side of the round pen to another. This movement, is in fact, another way of bonding for horses. Guiding a person, or horse, from one place to another, thereby directing movement allows one horse to lead another, and never does this become more important than in the presence of threats in the environment.

Effectively directing the escape of another horse from threats, is a way in which a deep bond between two horses is fostered. In Nimo's way, he was not only expressing affection for Casey's situation, but also trying to protect her from *further* harm. But also, by focusing his uninterrupted attention on her, he was practicing another integral facet of equine bonding, and that is, that in order to offer protection, the attention of one horse on another must be full and uninterrupted. A study conducted at Baylor University beautifully demonstrated this when dexamethazone, a sedative, was given to one member of a bonded pair of horses. The researchers measured the amount of times that the non-sedated horse approached the sedated one at the time of sedation, and then at one week, three week, and six week trials after the sedation. In a two hour period, under normal conditions, horses will approach one another roughly twelve times, yet when one of the two is sedated, the non-sedated horse will only approach five times. And this disruption in bonding appears to have lasting effects as after having his previous partner sedated, a horse will continue to be wary at 3 week and 6 week trials, approaching his former friend less than 7 times. Seemingly, when a horse's ability to be fully present, thereby attentive to the body movements of another horse, is disrupted, the bond between the two is not only immediately impaired, but remains so over time.

While the reasons for this complete attention and presence are dictated by survival needs, there is another very important factor that allows horses to avoid the distractions that would otherwise disrupt bonding. Because the bonding of horses is a physiological process, and not a conscious one, the connections horses do make, are *felt*, and not *thought*. This allows horses to respond to what is *unconscious* in people, as oppose to what is *conscious*. While Casey knew she was afraid, consciously, she had no idea that on an unconscious level, she was actually in a state of panic.

Relating on an unconscious level also means that horses respond to people's *needs*, not wants. While a person may consciously *want* the horse to come near, and may say so very clearly, I had witnessed many times, that horses reveal the many reasons that a person may *not* want the horse to come over. Another friend of mine, Sarah, who had purchased a horse, named Cappy, from me and was very determined that she wanted to compete the horse at high levels of dressage, and therefore, wanted more than anything to have a very close connection with him. Yet when turned loose in the round pen, Cappy would rarely approach Sarah, and when he did, would only stay for a moment, and then quickly move away, distracting himself by looking over the fence at the other horses, grabbing small scraps of hay from under the fence, and generally being disinterested. She would even try offering Cappy treats, grooming and rubbing him, but still he was hesitant to stay near her. When I asked Sarah why she needed to have closeness with Cappy, her response was that it would make her feel better. When I inquired again if it made her angry that what she thought she *needed* was not being given to her, she replied emphatically, "Yes." I asked further if this happens in other relationships, and after pausing in astonishment, she again answered, "Yes." While Sarah thought she needed the closeness of the relationship, it also was a source of frustration. When I finally asked if sometimes she *doesn't* want the relationship because it is too frustrating, she paused, and as if she had never considered the possibility before, and answered "Yes." While Sarah consciously wanted Cappy to come near, on an unconscious level, there was a part of her that did not. Cappy clearly was responding to what was unconscious for Sarah, and not what was conscious to her.

The reason that horses can remain completely attentive and present in relationships, where sometimes people will struggle, is because responding on an unconscious level, they do not "think" about relationships they way people do. *Therefore, rejections are not personalized.* This is always a concept that mystifies people. In teaching the process of "Join Up", defined by Monty Roberts, which involves pushing the horse away in order to begin a relationship with him, people who are new to horses are sure that the horse will see this as rejection and it will disrupt the development of a relationship. This is a perfect example, however, of how anthropomorphism disrupts our understanding of horses. Where being pushed away may be interpreted as rejection by a person, to a horse, it is an implied expression of freedom. By simultaneously signaling the horse to move away, and allowing him to do so, the non-verbal message is: *you can escape, I will not confine you, and you are free to go.* To a prey animal, whose survival depends on the ability to escape, this serves to *create*, not destroy, trust. To be sure, naturalistic observations of horses both in captivity and in the wild have recounted that after being pushed out of the herd by a dominant mare, a young horse will increase the amount of times he attempts to re-approach the mare. It seems that a "perceived" rejection, is in fact, all the more reason to re-approach, and these young horses often do so while displaying submissive behaviors, such as gaping the mouth, lowering the head, and positioning the body sideways in relation to the dominant mare. Unlike people, horses are *more* interested in another when there appears to be a lack of trust.

Looking down at General, with his head so comfortably encased in Kathy's arms, I asked, "So because Russell didn't trust them at first the herd was *more* concerned with him than with Sunday, who did trust them right away?"

"That's right."

"And they were more concerned because not trusting them made Russell unsafe?"

She scratched behind General's ears again, "Well no horse can survive alone. If Russell doesn't trust them, he will be alone, and this concerns them."

I looked over at Russell, now completely calm. The herd had begun to disperse a bit, having been reassured. I knew horses didn't isolate unless they were sick or dying, it is just they way they are. But I had thought they didn't isolate because they didn't *want* to. *But it was actually that the herd didn't want them too. They wouldn't let a horse isolate.* The more a horse isolated, the more the herd surrounded them. "There is no way a horse could attach by avoiding his emotions?" I asked, looking at Kathy. She was looking down at the top of General's head, lowered almost to her knees, completely relaxed.

She pulled her hands back from behind his ears and looked at me, "No. The herd wouldn't allow it."

Chapter Six

Where Does The Rage Go?

"Where does your rage go?' Dr. Heidel sat back in his chair and adjusted his tie. The cookie that had been "tempting him all day," now tempted me. *Anything to avoid answering that question.*

It took him eleven minutes to ask it. I had looked at my watch when his secretary apologized for tardiness, and assured me that it was no reflection of his desire to meet with me. "He has been very busy today. But he wants you to know, he does want to meet with you. If you can just be patient he will get to you." She leaned over me as I sat on the bench outside his office. *She must be a mom.* Either that, or she is used to assuring people waiting on Dr. Heidel.

"What?" I was buying time.

I had come to his office to ask about addiction. How it begins, what it does to people, and what happens if it is not treated. In searching for the answer to my question if avoiding emotions was a way of functioning at all, I discovered a new world. A vast community all focused on one thing. It affects every facet of the population, and aside from the war, is what the government spends the most amount of money treating, and cleaning up after. No longer do we associate it with skid row, but instead, Rush Limbaugh – and after his stay at the prestigious Sierra Tucson, many other celebrities as well. Addictions are now ubiquitous. About as common as the flu, I realized.

So when I contacted SAMHSA, the Substance Abuse and Mental Health Services Administration to ask who is considered the expert on addictions, little did I know, I would be asked about my rage.

"I asked you first." Dr. Heidel fixed his gaze on me.

"I don't know. I mean I didn't know I had rage." *Isn't that a bad word,* I thought to myself.

"Everybody does. It's a universal emotion."

"So I am supposed to have it?" I asked looking around his plush office. The carpet was a bright burgundy that accented the deep cherry trim and ornate desk that stood off to the left of the fireplace. The walls were adorned with sage colored curtains garnishing the massive windows that stretched up the length of the oversized walls. Everything in his office seemed overwhelming. The ceiling was twice as high as typical ceilings and gave the room a cathedral feel. The one hundred and eighty degree view of the Malibu coastline felt like it belonged on a postcard. I wondered if the office was designed to make people feel as if they were in a movie.

"You are not supposed to be afraid of it." Dr. Heidel noticed I had been looking around.

"What happens if you are?"

"I'll show you, follow me," Dr. Heidel stood and made his way toward the ornate double doors on the east wall of his office.

The treatment team meetings at Dr. Heidel's recovery center are a regular practice at all recovery centers. Some call them staff meetings. Some staff call them exhausting. Some patients say they are the staff conspiring against them. But as far as Dr. Heidel is concerned, they always begin with a prayer.

He adjusted himself in his chair and placed a small stack of papers on the armrest. "I just met with Suzan, our new patient. She came in last night, as a referral from Hazelden. She is the middle child in a family of five. She has an older sister by six years, and a younger brother by one and a half years. Her parents were immigrants from Iran, and came over here before having children. As a child, the patient recalls the mother being extremely critical and controlling. The father left the house when the patient was five years old, and mother never remarried. When the patient was 12, her older sister moved out, and from that point, the patient's mother became overly involved in her life, deciding everything from what she wore, to who she dated. She describes her decision to go to law school as a way to appease her mother," Dr. Heidel paused briefly and looked around the room.

Dr. Heidel continued on, "The patient started to struggle in her second year of law school, and began drinking. However, she kept her drinking hidden from the mother, and was able to make it through school and pass the bar. From there, she landed a position with a large firm, and did well, yet continued to drink. After two years at the firm, she decided to open her own firm, and took on a very high-powered client, who she depicts as very controlling, emotionally and verbally abusive. It was then that her drinking escalated. As the pressure from her client increased, she started drinking every night, and it finally got out of control when she was hospitalized for anxiety.

When the staff at the hospital, smelled alcohol on her, and tested her blood level at .12, they referred her to Hazelden. Hazelden then felt that she would be more appropriate for us, as she has severe rage."

Dr. Heidel took a breath and looked around the room. The seats were filled with counselors, therapists, a psychiatrist, a psychologist, a nurse, and the program director.

"Do we have the report from the hospital?" The program director looked over at the nurse.

"It's really bad." She flipped through a handful of papers on her lap.

"What does it say?" The program director picked up a pen from the armrest of her chair and began to write something on a piece of paper.

The nurse read from the paper in her hand. "Insomnia, migraines, dermatitis, allergies, irritable bowel syndrome, and ulcers, she's got about everything."

"Do we have the neuropsych on her?" the program director asked.

"Disruptions in conceptual thought, sequencing and organization of information, and short-term memory," Dr. Franz, the staff psychiatrist looked up from his lap. "She reminds me of what we used to see in Vietnam Vet PTSD cases. The anxiety level is so high, that the body starts attacking itself."

Dr. Franz would know. He was a Vietnam Veteran. He had spent two years as a corpsman in the military, treating contusions, burns, broken bones, malaria, and bullet wounds. And yet, despite helping numerous soldiers, and witnessing many more his was unable to help, he began to feel as though he was missing something. He could suture up the skin on a person and treat the infection pulsing through his body, yet he couldn't treat the torment racking his brain. At the time, very little was understood about PTSD, and even less was acknowledged. The military didn't want to admit that the damages a soldier suffered were anything but physical. The soldiers themselves were given an automatic discharge for so much as mentioning nightmares, and yet they had nowhere to go. There were virtually no recognized mental health programs offered to victims of war, and even psychiatry, with it's more traditional medical upbringings, was frowned upon. Yet the anguish on the faces, and panic, that didn't heal like physical wounds, was simply not something Dr. Franz could ignore. This is what he describes as the defining moment in his career. He was either going to ignore the mental anguish of the victims in front of him, as the military did, or he was going to try to understand them.

After completing his residency in psychiatry, he worked tirelessly to make the topic of mental health in the military discussable. And he walked with a limp. He too, had his battle scars. In that second year as a corpsman, while suturing up a patient, a piece of shrapnel from enemy fire lodged itself in his left hip, shattering it.

He shifted his position in his chair, and crossed his legs, "I'm going to start her on Seroquel and Respiridone to see if we can get that anxiety level down."

"Does the mother know she's here?" a voice called from across the room. Dr. Calvern, the trauma specialist, adjusted her glasses as she looked toward Dr. Heidel.

"No, and I'm glad you mentioned that," Jenice Contas, the intake director turned toward Dr. Calvert. "She was adamant that her mother not know she is here."

Dr. Arame, the psychologist, looked toward Dr. Heidel. A silent communication appeared to transpire. It wasn't the first time. Dr. Heidel had spent years under Dr. Arame. Working together from the time Dr. Heidel received his masters degree eighteen years ago, they had treated hundreds of cases. Between the two of them, there was no condition they hadn't seen.

"Mark my words," Dr. Heidel spoke slowly and deliberately, "if we don't get to her rage, she will not be able to stay sober."

I looked around the room. It was as if he had just said that there was a fire in the building.

"Her rage is going to kill her."

"It already is." Dr. Franz had seen this before too.

"You've to be very careful with this type of patient," Dr. Arame cleared his throat and adjusted his tie. "The issue of trust is a very delicate subject."

"If you force the issue of the mother too soon we will lose her." Dr. Heidel turned his gaze from Dr. Arame and looked across the room.

"It must be her choice to disclose the fact that she is here to the mother. She must first be able to talk about things that she doesn't trust about the therapist." Dr. Arame looked toward Dr. Calvert.

Dr. Heidel spoke assiduously, "The anxiety is a component of the fear of her rage. She is completely unaware of her rage at the mother. So she remains a victim to it. Because any fragile connection she has with people is dependent on containing her rage, it cannot be expressed outwardly. The medical report and the neuropsych tests are a reflection of that. That's what happens when rage remains unconscious."

Looking around the room, I realized that these were the people that the horses always avoided. In fact, they were afraid of them. A mare of mine who normally was quite social and calm had once gone into a complete panic while in the ring with a woman, who, the group she came with later told me, caused all of them to panic as well.

As the eight women witnessed my mare racing around the round pen frantically neighing, they had all looked at me, shocked, as the same mare had been half asleep with all of them. And although the woman was tense, there was something else, something underlying, that seemed to make those around her tense too. Yet my horse's reaction was beyond tense. She was terrified. What made it even more surprising was the fact that the woman didn't seem to be *doing anything* except for standing in the ring. She wasn't outwardly angry, screaming, yelling, or waving her arms, but my horse was desperately trying to get away from her. And yet, I had worked with many people who were outwardly angry, and not seen this sort of reaction from the horse. Many adolescents referred to me from the treatment center could be like this. The would come to the session making it clear that they didn't want to be there, be argumentative, and even violent at times. But the difference was these people *were* expressing their rage. We all, horses and people, knew it was there. And to a horse, when rage is expressed, it is readable, and therefore can be understood. The person, himself, who is expressing his rage can read and understand it, just like the adolescents that knew they were angry, is still able to respond to the emotions and behavior of the herd around him. Although these patients were always disruptive, they were able to communicate. Therefore, their rage does not disrupt the continuity of the herd. The problem then, with the woman, and rage that is not expressed, is that it is not conscious and therefore unreadable by the horse. This is rage that is felt, but not understood, meaning that it can go in any direction at any time, sort of like a ticking time bomb. But perhaps even worse, rage that is not conscious to a person also makes him unable to read and respond to the emotions of those around them. When I questioned my group about how responsive to their emotions they felt the woman was, they all replied that they felt a pressure to have things always be her way. In a a sense, the answer was not very. To a horse, this *is* something that disrupts the continuity of the herd. And while it was clear to me that this woman did have trouble understanding her own emotions and those around her, I would not have imagined this could predispose her to drinking.

Yet as Dr. Heidel spoke the words, "We must not let her leave here without expressing her rage, or she won't be sober," it became obvious that unexpressed rage did much more than just disrupt relationships.

Chapter Seven

They Say Get It Out

"**K**eeper!" I braced my weight against my stirrups and pulled hard on the reins. Keeper's head was halfway down, trying to get it between his knees. I couldn't let him -- it would be all over from there.

"Come on!" I cranked the left rein back, and stepped harder in the left stirrup. He spun around and came to a halt.

"God why does he have to do that?" I kept a tight feel on the reins. I wasn't sure he was done.

Bill stood grinning at me. He'd seen this before. Keeper was never one to avoid telling us how he felt about things. And usually in an exaggerated manner that involved a festive variety of bucking, bolting and leaping. My trusted coach walked over slowly and placing his cigarette in his teeth, reached up and took both reins in his hands. Keeper seemed to take a breath. He always liked Bill. "Do you know how to brace your reins?"

"No."

"You cross them over his neck and make an x." He pulled the left rein to the right across Keeper's neck, and pulled the right rein to the left making an x across the base of Keeper's neck. "They use it to stop them on the track."

"Okay," I sighed, "But why can't he just not do that?"

Bill stepped back, took the cigarette out of his mouth and dropped it in the sand, extinguishing it with his boot. "Horses don't work that way, especially this one."

"Why?"

"Do you remember what I told you about him on the track?"

Keeper had a lip tattoo, no race record, and no injuries. Horses are only given a lip tattoo when they enter their first race. It's the Jockey Club's way of tracking each horse's race record. As the overseeing organization of thoroughbred racing in the United States, they also use tattoos to prevent a sly trainer from swapping horses, and potentially making a boon off a racehorse that has been "dropped down" in class and now has a significant advantage over it's lesser counterparts. If a horse can't run without a tattoo, the trainer can't switch horses or alter race records. But Keeper had no race record. That means he never ran a race. Something happened between the morning of the race when he was given the tattoo, and the start of the race, later that afternoon. The usual conclusion would be that the horse had an injury that the trainer hadn't detected in the morning work, yet discovered in the process of grooming, saddling, or warming up for the race later that day. Yet Keeper had no injuries. Even if he had had a minor injury, and needed to be pulled from his first race, it is unlikely that he would've been sold as "sporthorse prospect," which is what the racehorse trainers call a horse that will never run again. Keeper's owner had paid too much money for him as a yearling at the Keeneland sale in Lexington, Kentucky. Between the one hundred and seventy five thousand dollar price and the year of training before his first race, it would've been too much to throw away for a minor injury. But the trainer had wanted him gone, which is what my agent told me when he arrived at the layup farm. Although he had managed to rub the trainer the wrong way, to me Keeper sounded exciting.

When I brought him home and showed him to Bill, his first question was where he came from. I explained the lip tattoo, the absent race record, the lack of injuries, and the sale price.

"He was carded," Bill smiled knowingly.

"What is that?" I asked suspiciously.

He paused as his adjusted his straw hat. "Means he can't go back to the track. That's why his papers are clean."

Almost every other horse I had gotten from the track had a stamp across his Jockey Club papers. The stamp read, "NOT FOR RACING." It is the trainer's way of preventing an enterprising trainer from trying to rehabilitate the horse and run him again. They do it because it wouldn't be fair. It wouldn't be fair to the owner, who bought the horse for a price exponentially higher than what he was sold for. To take a loss on a horse like that, the owner needs the small amount of consolation that not being taken advantage of brings. And it wouldn't be fair to the horse. They are usually sold when their injuries are too severe to allow future racing. It is the trainer's way of protecting the horse. It's also the trainer's way of protecting the horse when he is too slow. The tracks in Mexico are for the slow horses. But slow horses who don't bring in much money are not treated kindly. Not being regulated as stringently, if at all, as tracks in the US, the Mexican tracks are notorious for running horses into the ground. And there aren't rescue organizations and advocacy groups for the horse's life after racing in Mexico as there are in the States.

But a horse that has been carded doesn't need the stamp. He has been banned from returning to the track anyway. Somewhere between the morning tattoo, and the start of the race, Keeper did something horrible enough to warrant a ban. He could've kicked a race official, attacked another horse, or become violent at the gate. That was Bill's theory.

"Do you remember Del Mar?" Bill rested his arm on a jump standard.

I relaxed the rein a little on Keeper, and gave him an affectionate scratch on the neck. "How could I forget?"

I thought Keeper was going to kill me that day. We were next to go on the grand prix field, standing in between the stands and under the announcer's seat in the small tunnel that led to the field. With the solid walls on each side of us, the stands at eye level, and the roof overhead, it felt like a starting gate. The rider in front of us was only halfway through her course, and the rider behind us had started to sidle up behind. We were boxed in, and Keeper started to tense. Bill noticed and turned to the rider behind us, "Might want to give this one a little space. She didn't move. Keeper had already raised his head, shaking it side-to-side -- a telltale sign -- and now he was stepping nervously sideways. I braced stiffly with the expectation of an explosive energy that could go any direction. We couldn't enter the field, the rider wasn't finished with her course, and we had no room to back or sideways. He was going to go up. I couldn't feel it. It was the only way to go. Bill knew it too. "Go, push him forward."

"I can't, she's not done."

"You have too."

I nudged Keeper forward and shaking his head again, he projected forward into the ring, like a rocket launching into space. Catching him on the left rein, I quickly pulled him along the rail, in a feeble attempt to avoid disrupting the other rider's go. Keeper hopped and danced up and down, pitching forward. He wanted to go *now*. Looking back, I saw Bill speaking to the ring steward. You are *never* supposed to enter the ring before the rider in front of you has finished the course, *especially when leaping*. Entering too early could distract both the horse and the rider on the course, placing them at a significant disadvantage over the other riders. I said a silent prayer that Bill's influence would sway the ring steward and I wouldn't be eliminated.

I got the nod. The rider left the ring, and Bill had worked a miracle. In more ways than one. I couldn't hold Keeper anymore, and we bolted forward toward the first jump.

It made sense. Something had probably happened to him in the starting gate on the first race. He must have tried to do the only thing he knew how to do, to run. He was probably restrained, and when he couldn't run, fought back. So now, when he was in any situation that boxed him in, he fought back.

"But Keeper isn't boxed in right now. So why does he have to act angry?" I looked down at Keeper, his head now lowered sleepily and eyes fighting off an afternoon slumber.

"Because he is." Bill reached into his pocket and took out another cigarette.

"But why can't he just hold it in?"

"Horses don't work that way. When they are angry, it just comes out. It has to."

I looked across the arena toward the pastures. The three grassy runs all shared a fence line and stretched up the hill toward the back of the property. My parents had leased the ranch partially because it had so much pasture space. We used them mainly for broodmares and young horses, but we had also taken in a few boarders who wanted their horses out in pasture. The broodmares occupied the first, the boarders were in the middle and the young horses, three yearlings, were in the last pasture. "But why?"

"Who is the most dominant over there?" Bill followed my gaze and nodded toward the pastures.

"The mares, you mean?" I asked, watching Classic, Sylvie, and Zanzibar, the three broodmares, peacefully grazing in the afternoon sun. The small amount of grass that had been growing earlier in the year was now almost completely gone.

"Yeah."

"Definitely Classic."

"Okay, you want to see." Bill flicked the ashes from his cigarette and held it in his hand.

"See what?"

He took another drag from his cigarette, "Why horses can't hold in their anger."

"Yeah."

Bill started toward the pastures, "Follow me."

I nudged Keeper out of his slumber and pointed him toward the pastures.

Bill took one of the halters from the hook on the gate, "Will this fit her?"

"Classic?"

"Yeah."

I nodded.

Bill entered the pasture and shut the gate behind him. Sylvie, who was closest, turned to see who the unfamiliar intruder was. Bill reached down and picked up a handful of hay from the morning's feeding. Zanzibar, who stood next to Sylvie, started toward him. Classic, who was on the far side of the pasture had noticed, and came trotting over. As she neared Bill, Zanzibar, who was maybe twenty feet from Bill, noticed and stopped. Classic rushed by her, and she stepped to the side. Sylvie hung back.

Bill gave Classic the small amount of hay in his hand and reached up and put the halter on. Classic walked eagerly next to Bill as he led her out of the gate. Sylvie and Zanzibar came up behind, curiously. Classic lifted a hind leg. They quickly backed away.

Bill led her up the hill toward the last pasture. As he passed the pasture with boarders, they came running up to the fence, interested in what was going on. Classic turned her haunches toward them as they poked their noses over the fence. With a squeal, she lifted a hind leg toward them, and they backed away. Reaching the yearlings, Bill shooed them back away from the gate and led Classic in. He then took the halter off and let her go. The three yearlings quickly surrounded her sniffing every part of her body. Immediately she squealed and whirled. She pinned her ears flat against her head, and pointed it straight out, giving her the look of a snake. Then she spun and aimed her haunches at them, as they scurried off. She then proceeded to check the pasture, starting with the ground, sniffing it for any last scraps of hay, and then marching directly toward the small grain buckets hanging on the fence. She deliberately checked them one by one. As she did, Bien Vida, her foal from last year, and also the most dominant of the yearlings, came over. She approached the bucket Classic had just finished inspecting. Just as she began to stick her nose in it, Classic came flying over, teeth barred, and ears pinned. Bien Vida saw her just it time, and spun away, narrowly missing her mother's teeth. Classic checked the bucket again, then turned and headed toward the water trough on the far side of the pasture. The yearlings, who had been huddled together against the fence, all scattered away. Classic sniffed the trough, and then turned back toward the gate. The remnants of the morning's feeding collected on the ground just in front of the gate. Classic sniffed them again and then turned to look back at the yearlings. They were gathered together under the small shade directly opposite the gate.

Bill, who had been standing at the gate watching Classic complete her rounds, entered the pasture with something in his hand. From where I was sitting on Keeper's back I couldn't tell what it was. My eyes had been fixed on Classic, and I hadn't noticed him pick anything up.

He closed the gate behind himself and walked slowly toward Classic. She had been watching him from the time he opened the gate. The yearlings all looked in his direction too.

Bill opened his hand and with a flick of his wrist, fluttered a white plastic grocery bag with air. Classic jerked her head up, snorted loudly and took off running. Bill walked a few steps after her and shook the bag again. The yearlings all huddled close together and backed up against the fence. Bill was directly across the pasture from them, and there was nowhere to go. They were as far away as possible. He stopped and stood still slowly rattling the bag. They backed further, nervously snorting, and looking back and forth from each other to the bag. Jostling for places, each one tried to move furthest from Bill. He kept shaking the bag. Classic, who had run to the water trough in the far corner of the pasture stood backed against the fence as well. She snorted and looked around for a place to go. She called to Sylvie and Zanzibar. Noticing the commotion they had also run to the far corner of their pasture. They stood huddled together under the shade cover next to the gate. They too, were as far away from Bill as possible. But they called back. Classic called again, circled around, and butted her chest against the fence that separated them. She looked nervously at Bill, and back at Sylvie and Zanzibar.

The three boarder's horses, in the middle pasture, had taken off running at the same time as everyone else. They too, stood huddled against the fence, as far away from Bill as possible, butting up against the fence. When Classic called to Sylvie and Zanzibar, they also called back.

Bill shook the bag once more. Classic looked toward Sylvie and Zanzibar and called again. Again they called back. The boarders also called back. And now the yearlings called too. Classic nervously searched around. First she looked to Sylvie and Zanzibar, then back at Bill, then to the boarders, then back at Bill, and finally to the yearlings. Bill shook the bag again. Classic looked at him, and then the yearlings. He shook again, and again she looked. And then she took a few steps. Hesitantly, she moved toward the yearlings. Keeping her body tight against the fence, she turned her head back and forth from Bill to them. Bill shook the bag again. Classic took one last anxious glance at Bill and bolted for the yearlings.

As she came flying under the shade cover, the yearlings made way for her. Coming to a sliding stop she almost ran right into them. But this time, they didn't move away. Instead they huddled around her. She nervously sniffed their necks and backs. They sniffed back. She looked toward Bill. He shook the bag again. She immediately moved in closer to the yearlings. They hadn't noticed and remained preoccupied with sniffing her. Bill shook again. Again she moved in closer, and again the yearlings didn't notice. Bill slowly stepped back and began to wad the bag up in his hand. Classic kept a wary eye on him. He tucked the bag into a pocket in his jacket and backed all the way to the gate. Classic slowly lowered her head and sniffed the yearlings again. They hadn't left their tight positions next to her. Bill opened the gate and walked out of the pasture. Classic watched him as he made his way back toward Keeper and I.

"What was that?" I picked up the reins again and stroked Keeper's neck.

"What was the first thing she did?" Bill stopped to rest his arm on the fence.

"She pushed them all away."

"How did she do that?" Bill leaned back and adjusted his hat.

"Well, by being angry at them."

"And then what happened?"

"What, when you shook the bag?"

"Yeah," Bill nodded.

I looked over at Classic, now pleasantly munching hay with the yearlings nearby, "Well they all spooked at the bag."

Bill took off his glasses and proceeded to clean them. "Right, and where did she run to?"

"To the corner, by herself."

"Okay, and then what?"

I looked again at the three yearlings, standing perfectly calm as if nothing had happened. "Well she finally ran to them."

"What was she looking for when she ran to them?" he asked putting his glasses back on.

"Well protection I guess."

"Did she find it?"

I looked at her again. You would never know she was terrified only minutes before. "Looks like it."

Bill grinned slightly, "So why didn't she hold in her anger?"

"I guess she didn't need to."

I thought about the many times I had wished Keeper could hold his anger in. All the while I never knew I was wanting him to do something he had no need to do. Anger in horses doesn't inhibit protection, the way it does in people. *So horses can't repress their anger because there is no need to.*

I knew about horses that they respond to needs and not wants. And for them, they are often one in the same. Many horses I had worked with in the past may have appeared to "want" something, such as to leave the arena, but really it was what they *needed* to do. And in the times I had responded to these equine needs, the horses had always calmed down. In my years of riding, I had always described this as an instinctive sense. When a horse needs to buck you let him go -- *especially when he's angry.* Many of the racehorses I had worked with could be this way, often becoming infuriated when a whip is raised, or when held tightly by the reins. And if you fight them, their rage is escalated. Yet if you allow it, and accept it, the way horses do, they calm down.

But I had also witnessed many unskilled trainers attempting to *train the rage* out of horses. The minute the horse would pin his ears back, or raise a hind leg, the trainer would whip him harshly. Yet instead of extinguishing the behavior, the trainer's reprimands would only invoke more teeth grinding, kicking, and ear pinning. Many horses can be ruined this way. For if this goes on long enough, the horse will simply shut down, becoming apathetic and unresponsive to *any* cues. A stallion I had gotten off the track had come to me this way. While I had been told that he was hit a lot at the track, I had underestimated the effect this might have had on him. The first time I attempted to ride him, he simply went backward. I closed my leg, giving him the cue to go forward, and instead, he raised his head and backed up. I tapped with the whip, and he clenched his teeth and backed further. The more I squeezed with the leg, or tapped with the whip, the more he backed. This went on for days, until, finally, I discovered that he was still responsive to visual cues. If I held the whip out to the side and shook it, he'd go forward. For this horse, he had been fought with so much that he had become completely ignorant of a riders cues, and the only way to get through to him was to use cues that hadn't already been ruined. But this meant also tolerating his anger.

Because expressing any emotion -- even anger -- is a hallmark of herd dynamics, and the herd itself, represents safety, asking a horse to contain or extinguish his emotions jeopardizes his safety. In a sense, he is wise to fight against it. What humans often interpret as a horse's selfish wants are really their primal needs. But horses also have *no reason* to contain their rage as people do. No matter how much anger a horse expresses at another, the herd will still protect him. And horses do not make judgements on behavior the way people do. To a horse, behavior always has a need, and is therefore accepted for that reason. Where people may categorize behavior as bizarre, crazy, or inappropriate, horses simply accept behavior as necessity -- regardless of the nature of it.

So my wanting Keeper to choose more appropriate times to express his anger wasn't something he could respond to. It was *my* need and not his. His often, explosive episodes were his way of expressing that he needed to feel safe. And maybe it was my rage he was really responding to – expressing it in the only way he could. Although I'd wished for something other than his explosions, asking him to repress them would have actually made him feel less safe.

Unlike in people, rage in horses doesn't destroy relationships. *So horses don't need to repress their rage to maintain connection.*

Chapter Eight

Mistrust

"Does the patient know his delusions are not reality?" Dr. Arame's face looked strained. Squinting his eyes a little, he was trying to understand something that was not particularly comprehensible.

Neither had my patient been. He would shift around in his chair, swiveling his head, backwards, left, right. He couldn't check behind himself enough to be satisfied. He'd ask questions about those "things" behind him. "What are they doing?"

"Who?" I'd respond. He'd shift around and only half look at me. Then he'd stand and pace around. "Do you want to go somewhere?" I'd ask tentatively.

"Stupid Commi's, they've got my mom?" His hands shook with anger.

"The Commi's have your mom?" Another half glance. No answer. Then he'd turn and try to climb the wall. He loved to rock climb.

"Who has your mom?" I leaned forward in my seat.

"Why does the food here have so much fat in it?" Still scaling the wall, his lean frame took on the shape of a spider. He hated fat. Anything fat, fat people, fat food, fat animals. Two days ago, he had been ranting about the permanent resident, Sally's dog. She'd been innocently feeding him steak and cheese in the community kitchen. But this infuriated my patient. The dog was too fat. He didn't want it anywhere near him. And why did it have to be so fat? He'd become fixated.

"What is it about fat that bothers you so?" I had queried.

"My mother is too fat," he looked behind himself nervously, as if expecting to be attacked by a fat person.

"Does she make you nervous?" I had tried to keep eye contact with him.

He stood up, "Turn it off," he screamed at the field workers down the hill. They were running a Punjab, and it was too loud. I had thought sitting outside might be more comfortable for him. But instead, he had gotten fixated on the Punjab.

This was how our sessions had been going. Feeling as perplexed as my client appeared to be, I had requested to meet with Dr. Arame.

But actually, I didn't call him Dr. Arame. I called him Gio, short for Giovanni. I don't know if anyone actually called him Dr. Arame. That was just how the program director referred to him when she wanted him to call a patient's parents. It made him sound more professional I suppose. Or maybe it was his thick Italian accent that seemed to command reverence. For the rest of us, it was his brilliance we sought. Secretly, we probably all wanted to be like Gio, especially the accent.

Dr. Arame was born in Italy and his entire family was still there. Although his parents didn't attend college, he'd been fascinated with the inner working of the human mind from early on -- perhaps in a way to understand himself better. The youngest among a family of five, his father had been a military officer and his mother had tried to make up for his absence in the way a doting Italian mother does. Yet there was little to make up for. His father compensated by making each return an exciting event. He'd organize games, outings, and "excursions" for the children, all centered around laughter. He was quiet himself, a reserved, circumspect man. Perhaps it was he who wanted the laughter as much as his children. It was all he could do. The only discharge from the military came in the form of broken bones, as there was no such thing as a "psychiatric discharge." Perhaps he had considered it -- I'd often wondered where Dr. Arame's innate sensitivity for psychosis came from. He was prophetic in that way.

He had been trained at the famous Milan school in Italy specializing in that subset of the Diagnostic and Statistical Manual for Psychiatric conditions that most of us stray away from. Conditions like schizophrenia, dissociative fugue, and dementia, were their specialties at a time when treatment of them usually meant locking them away. When Dr. Arame emigrated to the United States in 1970, the year after the California Mental health Act of 1969, they had only just been released. The Act was a game change in the world of mental health. It read that, "those suffering from psychiatric conditions can no longer be involuntarily confined without appropriate grounds." That meant a psychiatric evaluation that began with a seventy-two hour hold that could only be extended when the patient remained a danger to himself or others. Despite public fear of these people, they could no longer be permanently segregated. Dr. Arame didn't know it, but at the time he settled in Los Angeles, may of them had collected there, as the weather was conducive to the homeless state they found themselves in. Although the act gave them freedom, it didn't give them help. And they were not prepared to take care of themselves as they had been institutionalized for much too long to develop the skills necessary for functional lives. Worse, many of their families had turned their backs on them, in an expression of not so much misunderstanding as fear. Maybe it was Dr. Arame's intuition that brought him there.

I'd come to know him through the treatment center I was working for at the time. As the center specialized in pervasive conditions, we received a lot of referrals from other treatment centers. Every time another center had a patient that they couldn't figure out, they sent him to us. Whether they knew it or not, it was Dr. Arame who understood them, not us. He only proffered the information.

"I can't tell what he thinks, Gio," I turned my hands over in exasperation and sat back in the overstuffed chair on the right side of the room, the same chair I always took in the weekly treatment team meetings. During these meetings, each therapist would present his/her clients to be discussed, and the treatment methods used would be examined. The founder, a self-made millionaire of French descent with an intolerance for error, would question the efficacy of the treatment, and essentially, the therapist. In the worst cases, he would make an example of your error. A public example of *what not to do*. For a young therapist, the meetings were like throwing yourself out to the wolves.

Each of us had our own chair that we preferred. The program director across from the founder, the seasoned therapists against the wall on the left side of the room, the most seasoned therapist next to the founder, and the young therapists in the corners. My corner chair was closest to the door, which is why I preferred it. Whenever I felt this way with a patient, I fantasized making a quick exit.

We had decided to meet in this room because Dr. Arame didn't have an office. Although he never so much as mumbled discontentment, I always thought he should.

He turned and sat in the chair to my left, the one usually occupied by the founder. Dr. Arame never took a regular chair, as it wouldn't suit his casually late entrance. He'd stroll in with a Starbucks in his hand and we'd all look around to make sure that he had a space to sit in. Leaning back in the chair, he rested his arms on the armrests, tilted his head slightly downward and said nothing. *Explain yourself.*

"I know he doesn't like fat." The center had wanted me to evaluate him for an eating disorder. From the time he'd arrived, he'd been separating his food, picking at it, sliding it around his plate, and for the most part, avoiding eating. "I know he looks behind himself a lot, He gets up and paces, and sometimes tries to climb the walls." I paused, trying to figure out the best way to describe my patient. "No matter what I do, he won't hold eye contact with me."

Dr. Arame moved his hand from in front of his mouth. He usually kept it placed there when listening intently. "Does he trust you?"

I hadn't thought much behind trying to keep him in one place long enough to speak with him. Whether or not he trusts me, I hadn't had time enough to consider. "Gio, I have no idea. Well," I thought back to his angry outbursts. He had never been angry at me, just the things around him, "he gets angry a lot, but not at me."

"Who does he get angry at?" Dr. Arame adjusted his tie.

I looked out the window directly across from me. It was an incredible view of the Malibu coastline. The workers just down the hill were still running the Punjab, "Mostly anyone who seems to disrupt things around him. You know, like loud noises, sudden movements, things like that."

"He doesn't trust his environment."

I wasn't sure if he was asking a question, or providing an observation. "No, definitely not." I hadn't thought of that either. "But Gio, how does a person get to be that way?"

A slight upturn of the corner of his mouth gave him away. He loved to explain, but would only offer if first asked. "The relationship with the mother is crucial."

Dr. Arame was going to make me continue asking questions, that's the way he was, "How does that make a person not trust his environment?"

He kept his gaze fixed on me, crinkling his eyes in a very discerning, yet soft expression, "Have you asked the patient about whether his mother accepts him?"

Although I had never asked my patient directly, his mother had shared her version of what her son should be doing with me. "Well, no, she has her own ideas for him."

"Do you have an example?"

"Well, she wants him to go to college, and he wants to teach rock climbing." I pictured my patient assessing the wall for handholds just the day before. I, too, had thought it was odd, yet it was clearly what he loved to do. In fact, it occurred to me that rock climbing was the only thing I could keep him focused on. He literally became electric when he talked about it. As far as his mother was concerned, however, it was a dangerous and unsophisticated activity. "Oh, and the mother thinks he is too skinny."

"How does she respond when he expresses his own ideas?"

I thought back to the conversations I had had with my patient's mother. "She shuts him down," I paused, "the same way she does to me."

Dr. Arame raised an eyebrow, "What is the feeling you get when she shuts you down?"

"Me?" I looked toward the door.

He didn't waiver, "Yes."

"Well, I feel angry."

"And how does she respond to that?"

I shifted in my seat, "I don't tell her that I feel angry."

Dr. Arame looked at me inquisitively, "Why not?"

The skin on the back of my neck went cold, "Gio, she kinds of makes me nervous." I thought back to the weekly phone calls I had to make to her. Although I was reporting on her son's progress, or apparent lack thereof, I felt as I was being evaluated.

He remained absolutely still, "In what way?"

My eyes darted around the room. It occurred to me that I was acting as my patient had been, "I get the feeling that she is going to explode if I don't say the right thing."

Dr. Arame had noticed me looking around the room, "So you become afraid of expressing anger."

"Yeah, I don't think it would go well."

"What could it look like if it doesn't go well?"

I thought back to our first conversation. She had grilled me about the treatment, my expertise, and what we could do to "fix" her son. I felt as if I had to say what she wanted to hear. "Well, the relationship wouldn't be the same, I mean, she might not talk to me after that."

He pulled his hand from in front of his mouth, "It would destroy the relationship?"

"Yes." As I replied, I realized that we really didn't have much of a relationship to begin with.

"So keeping the relationship depends on avoiding your anger," he raised his chin and kept his eyes on me, "Do you trust the mother?"

I hadn't thought about that either, "No."

"So your patient must have never learned to trust his mother."

It hadn't occurred to me what had been happening. *If I felt as though I couldn't trust the mother, how could my patient?*

"Wait, I leaned forward in my chair, "so because he has not ever been able to express his anger at his mother, he hasn't learned to trust her?"

He nodded his head forward slowly, "That's right."

"But then what does that have to do with trusting the environment?"

The same slight upturn appeared in the corner of Dr. Arame's mouth, "We learn how to trust from the mother."

"The environment too?"

"The concept of trust."

No wonder my patient couldn't trust his environment. He had never learned *how* to trust. "So he never learned the concept of trust, at all."

Dr. Arame smiled. It was clear to him what was happening, "Exactly."

Dr. Arame wasn't the only one who understood my client. Clients such as mine always captivate horses. They follow them around, entranced, and almost as if put under a spell. Consistently horses show more interest in clients with thought disorders, such as schizophrenia, than any other type of client. And it isn't necessarily concern. Instead, there's a calmness that falls over horses when with these people, and they can get them to do things that they never would with others.

As schizophrenics are much more sensitive to their environment, and more prone to hypervigilance, their thinking is like that of horse. In fact, they do much less thinking, and much more feeling. Where the average person may miss subtle social cues, such as a deflection of the eyes, these are the very things that cause a schizophrenic, and a horse, to startle. What sometimes is a wedge in human relationships, therefore, can bind the relationship between a person with a thought disorder and a horse. And as the horse, who depends on hypervigilance to maintain his safety, understandably, feels contained by the schizophrenic, he develops a magnetic-like attachment to him. The schizophrenic is just as attentive to and concerned about the environment as the horse is, leading to a kinship -- two thinking and responding on the same level. In this way, trust between a horse and a schizophrenic extends beyond just where the horse is comfortable, and to areas of the horse's environment where he is unsure, or afraid. A young male client of mine had once attended a therapy group where the focus of the group was to work effectively with the large, bullheaded, draft horse to establish a communication that allowed for directional changes. Essentially, the clients were trying to get the massive Shire gelding to go both ways of the small round pen, and change direction on command. Yet, despite their numerous attempts, the horse would simply back up and shaking his head, attempt to scare the clients. And scared they were, for each one of them had gone running out of the ring at this. Yet when my 24 year old male schizophrenic entered the ring, the Shire, who had been standing as far as possible from the gate and avoiding any contact whatsoever, came over. The 18 hand horse lowered his head to the young man and keeping it softly planted on his back, proceeded to follow him around the ring. The horse, who had looked for all the world to be dangerous, now appeared completely docile. While my client walked about the ring, changing direction several times, the horse never once looked away. Instead, he was completely transfixed, and put into a state of calm willingness.

Because of the way schizophrenics "feel" the world around them, they offer containment to horses in a way that unaffected people simply can't. And for those who suffer from thought disorders -- autism, aspergers, schizophrenia, and dissociative fugue -- horses offer a containment that people are not equipped to.

I leaned farther forward and balanced my elbows on my knees, "So, Gio, what do I do?"

He looked down and positioned his tie, "You have to teach him how to trust."

I looked out the huge wall of windows across from me. Two tiny sailboats were making their way across the ocean, their white sails like flags on the water. "How do I do that?"

"You begin with all the things he doesn't trust about you," he gently waved his hand as he spoke, as if fanning air up toward his face.

The two sailboats moved slowly, the huge blue expanse opening up in front of them, appearing endless, "You mean I ask him to talk about what about me he doesn't trust?"

"Yes."

"How will that help?"

Dr. Arame kept his soft eyes on me, "You have to join with him in his mistrust. Right now, he is alone in his suspiciousness, which makes it worse. When this happens, his delusions will become more severe because he is not able to talk about them."

I thought back to the "things" he'd asked about. In his own way, he was asking to talk about them. "So his delusions stem from his inability to trust?"

"Yes," he spoke slowly, "because he can't trust *this* reality, he has created his own."

"And then he retreats to it when he feels as if he cannot trust the world around him." *No wonder he wanted to scale the walls,* I thought to myself.

"Exactly."

"So I have to retrieve him from it." *Sort of like a human rescue.*

His chiseled face eased a bit, "That's the only way he can learn to trust."

Chapter Nine

They Know More Than Us

"Did you tell them he's a weaver?" Sandi slammed the brakes on the golf cart and it skidded to a stop.

Lowering my weight into the saddle, I closed my hands on the reins, bringing the young three year old I'd been hacking to a halt. "He's not."

She stood and placed her hands on her hips, "Oh yes he is, come see."

If there was one thing I had learned about Sandi in the three months I'd been riding for her, it was not to question her. There was no need to, she'd been right about everything so far, even when I was absolutely sure she was wrong. I should've known better, Sandi had spent a lifetime around horses.

Growing up on the east coast, she had her start in horses like so many kids do, through the local pony club. Only there was one problem, she had no pony. Struggling financially themselves, there was just no way her parents could afford her passion. "See if someone will lend you a horse," was their response. Sandi did find someone willing to barter the privilege of riding their pony in exchange for feeding and mucking out the pony's corral twice a day. Even though she had to bike five miles to and from their house twice a day, and get up at five am to be at school in time, Sandi thought she had struck gold. That is, until she tried to ride the pony. What the family hadn't told her was that the only reason the pony was being lent out in the first place, was because their daughter refused to ride him.

He had bucked, bolted, and attempted to dislodge her by aiming for low hanging branches at a full gallop. When he tried the same routine with Sandi, she quickly realized that the "sweet little pony," she'd been caring for was a demon in disguise. But she refused to give up. The only way she was going to have a pony to ride, was to learn how to ride this one. And for Sandi, giving up was not an option. That's what made her such a great rider. Graduating from the ranks of pony club, and moving to a larger hunter-jumper barn, Sandi's name soon became associated with an uncanny ability to ride anything with four legs. *Especially ponies.* Because she was young and still quite small, ponies that had outsmarted their naive young riders were sent to her, as the adult trainers were typically too heavy for them. A typical problem with kids and ponies, and much of the reason ponies have a reputation for being malicious, this situation is also what makes a fearless kid rider invaluable.

But it wasn't just fearlessness that led to Sandi's success. Due much more to necessity than anything else, she learned how to read the horses. Subtle movements often missed by other riders' became second nature to her. Before long, she could almost predict what each horse was going to do, before he did it. And she knew how to respond to them too. Where other riders would leap off in fear, or resort to whips and spurs in anger, Sandi would sit quiet, and do nothing. At least that is what it looked like. Yet, she was communicating, imperceptibly, with each horse. Sometimes she'd move quickly and forcefully with the horse, but never against him, and never in anger.

When she decided to move to California and start her own training business, after years fluctuating between the hunter jumper circuit and the racetrack on the east coast, she soon found herself with more horses than she could take on. At the time, not many other trainers would take on the projects she would, and none were quite as effective. Adding to her talent was the fact that she specialized in sales, and knew most of the trainers on the east coast. A horse that had developed a bad reputation in California, could get a fresh start at a barn across the country. In effect, with Sandi's talent and connections, he could be taken from a horse that "no one wants" to a valuable asset.

"You weren't kidding," I hopped down from the young mare and ran my stirrups up. Sure enough, the horse I had brought in for Sandi's buyers to see was swaying back and forth in what seemed like a half conscious state. Eyes glazed over in a fixed stare at nothing in particular, he looked like a zombie.

"You didn't tell them?" Sandi rested her hand on my horse's gate and shifted her weight as she looked at me incredulously. If there was one thing Sandi would never sacrifice to make a sale, it was the truth.

I shook myself from the hypnotic state I was in, and shifted my eyes back to Sandi, "I didn't know. I didn't even know what weaving was."

Sandi, turned her head back toward my horse, "You've never seen a weaver before?"

"No. How does a horse get like that?" I asked taking in a behavior that I had only seen before in autistic children.

"It's a man-made condition," she turned back toward the golf cart and sat down.

"You mean, it doesn't happen in the wild?" I turned loosening the girth on the young mare.

She sat back against the seat and put her hand on the steering wheel, "It doesn't happen until we create it."

I looked back at my horse, still bobbing slowly side-to-side. "Why not?"

"Hop in," she patted the seat of golf cart and I sat next to her, pulling the mare along side. She sped down the barn aisle as the mare trotted beside   us, "You met Junior?"

I handed the mare off to Arturo, her groom, "No, who's that?" I asked turning back toward her.

"You'll see." She turned the cart toward the back pastures that stretched out down the hill behind the huge unfenced arena. Typically used to raise the young and rest the old, the back pastures were also a place for the horses Sandi didn't want her buyers to see. Sliding the cart to a stop again, she reached behind her seat and pulled a halter out of the tangled pile that created a mound on the back shelf of the golf cart. Watching her as she upended the mound, a movement to my left caught my eye. A solid black horse, nose against the fence, was bobbing and weaving rhythmically in the catch pen that stood in the corner of the pasture. Sandi used catch pens for horses that had learned to evade people and turned catching them into a chore. A horse that became evasive with people in a pasture, would go running the moment he saw the halter. And once he learns this method of escaping, it could be almost impossible to halter him. However horses only learn to run from the halter, when there is a reason to.

"That him?" I nodded toward the shiny black gelding.

Sandi nodded back, "Not bad looking, huh?"

I turned back toward Junior, his rhythmic sidestepping creating a flume of dust on each side, "No, but what happened to him?"

She pulled her gloves on and started toward angled corner of the wooden catch pen, "He came from a dressage barn at LAEC, and the owner refused to turn him out because she was worried he'd hurt himself." She paused at his gate, the dust cloud billowing up behind her, "so from the time he was imported at three, he was boxed up, and only saw the light of day when the trainer rode him. But because they didn't turn him out, he go to play, and scare the trainer who'd then just crank on him more and put him in draw reins."

The LAEC stood for the Los Angeles Equestrian Center, but actually, I might as well have stood for a zoo. Sitting in the heart of the city, the ambiance is complimented by freeways, smog and loud noises. And like Los Angeles, it's overcrowded. Like people, horses that live there have been known to become neurotic. Especially when they are imported from Europe where the farms are typically pastoral and quiet, horses are completely unprepared for the mayhem they find themselves in. Draw reins are a way to run a separate rein from either between the horses front legs, or attached to the girth of the saddle under the rider's stirrups, like a pulley system that forces the horse's head into a correct position. While this can give the trainer added control, it also forces the head into an unnatural position, and many horses soon come to resent them. "So not only did he only see the light of day when being ridden, but even then, he had to stare at the dirt."

Sandi shook her head. She hated lack of understanding leading to abuse, even if it came in the sophisticated version. "It's a shame-could've been a nice horse," she opened the gate.

I hadn't stopped watching him weaving-he seemed completely unaware that we were there, "So how long has he been like that?"

She approached slowly, swinging the rope lightly in his direction, "About a year -- they tried everything from stall toys to music -- he hasn't responded to anything."

"That's why he's in here?"

Junior hadn't responded to the Sandi, and she reached up to scratch his neck, "Yeah, I was worried he'd run straight into the fence, he seemed so out of it."

I watched her slide the rope slowly over his neck and pull him toward her, "So what are you going to do with him?"

She moved to his left side and slid the halter over his nose, "I'm going to put him with the mares."

Sandi's broodmares were like the school board members that liked to believe that they really ran the school. They had been here the longest, and seemed to think they'd earned the right. A bossy set of old thoroughbreds, warmbloods, and a few quarter horses Sandi frequently used them to reprimand the young geldings when they got out of line. She'd put an unruly youngster in with them and he would come out a polite, penitent animal, ready to work. I followed her as she made her way down the hill toward their pasture.

As we approached their pasture, the mares came running up to the fence. Junior still looking dazed, and didn't seem to notice. Pausing at the gate, Sandi turned back toward me. In my haze I had forgotten to step inside the pasture and drive the mares back away from the gate so she could enter. "Sorry," I grabbed a rope off the back of the cart and hustled through the gate. Driving the mares back, I turned to check that Sandi had let Junior loose, and slid through the fence out of the pasture.

Junior stood facing us where Sandi had left him. Right as the mares rushed him, suddenly, another movement on my right side caught my eye. Tucker, Sandi's German Shepard was racing toward us. Known for his proclivity for chasing horses, Sandi usually separated him from them. Only two years old, any moving object from a tennis ball to a visitor's car meant a potential hunt. Becoming fixated, he'd go into a frenzy until Sandi called him off. Turning back toward her, I touched her arm and pointed, "There's Tucker." She nodded, keeping her eyes fixed on the horses.

I stood back as Tucker flew past us in a whir. Ducking through the gate, he headed toward the group of horses that had encircled Junior. They all wheeled around and took off. Except for Junior. He seemed oblivious to the fact that the mares had bolted toward the other side of the pasture. Expecting him to run, Tucker had missed it too. In mid stride, he caught a glance of Junior, halted, and spun back toward him. Reaching Junior in three strides, he pounced at him, both front feet hitting the ground almost underneath the massive black body. Lunging from side to side, he barked nervously pounding the ground with his feet. But Junior stood still, seemingly unresponsive to Tucker's flurry of barks and pounces. Eyes glazed over, he looked like a deer in headlights. Becoming crazed, Tucker crouched lower as he aimed and snapped at Junior's heels. Lunging forward and backward, each thrust came dangerously closer to contact. Yet Junior was frozen in place.

I looked over at Sandi. She too, was motionless, her eyes locked on the commotion.

A neigh from the back of the pasture caught my attention. The mares, who had been watching the commotion, all stood facing Junior. Ears pricked forward, and heads raised, they were as focused on Junior and Tucker as Sandi was. Looking toward each other and then back toward Junior, they began to rustle. One of them gave another neigh, stepped forward, and paused, looking back at the herd. Then another mare stepped forward and reached out, touching her nose to her companion's flank. Another neigh, and a different mare moved from the herd also reaching out to the first with her nose. Taking another few steps forward, the mare in front neighed again. It was Divine, Sandi's best mare, and also the most dominant. With each step forward she paused, hesitantly, and the two mares flanked her just a step behind. The rest of the herd stood back, a tight bunch collected in the corner of the pasture. Stepping and pausing, Divine began to pick up speed. She trotted a few steps and paused again, lowering her head and snorting. The two mares hung back. Then suddenly, she galloped forward, lowered her head, and flattened her ears completely back. Aiming right at Tucker, she hit him at full speed. He went flying to the side and landed skidding sideways. He immediately came racing back at her. She spun and wheeled her hind end at him sending a flurry of kicks in his direction. He dodged her kicks and went right for Junior. Divine cut him off, bumping right into Junior's side with her chest. The stunned gelding lurched sideways, and struggled for balance. Unfazed by Divine, Tucker leapt at him again. Lunging in front of the now furious dog, Divine sent Junior staggering to the side again. As he tried to steady himself, Divine nipped, hitting him first on the rump, and then the shoulder. Tucker went for Junior again, and again Divine bumped him forward, determinedly driving her teeth into the black hide. He lurched a few steps forward. Divine kept her body between the unsteady black mass and Tucker, nipping him forward while kicking at Tucker. Junior lurched forward again. She nipped again, sending him forward a few more steps. She was driving him toward the two mares that had flanked her, and with each nip he steadied more, and picked up speed. Finally he broke into a trot. As Junior approached them, they circled around beside him and nudged him forward. Divine then spun toward Tucker and caught him on the shoulder with her teeth, sending him flying again. Turning back toward Junior, she rushed up behind him and drove him into the herd. They all gathered around, sniffing the shiny black coat from head to toe. Junior began to sniff back tentatively. Fifteen noses sniffed and nuzzled back. Standing encircled by them, he took a step toward Divine. She greeted him with a soft nuzzle, then moved away. He took another step toward a different mare, and she reached out with her nose, touching him along the neck. Then another mare, and another -- slowly, he was beginning to wake up. Tucker, on the other hand, had finally retreated, and was standing next to the golf cart, panting.

"That answer your question?" Sandi turned toward me.

Still mesmerized, I kept my eyes on the herd, "About weaving?"

She reached up shielding her eyes from the sun, "About why it doesn't happen until we create it."

"You mean because Tucker went after Junior?" I turned toward her.

"Why do you think he went after him?"

I looked over at Tucker, now lying beside the golf cart, "Because he was an easy target?"

"Well," she put her hands on her hips, "what made him an easy target?"

I glanced back over at Junior, "He was out of it."

"Exactly," she answered as if that solved the mystery.

"So wait," I looked back at Sandi, "weaving doesn't happen in the wild because it makes the horse vulnerable to prey?"

She nodded toward the group of mares gathered around Junior, "Not just the horse, the herd."

"What do you mean?"

She turned back toward them, "Did you notice what Divine did?"

"Yeah, she came over and defended Junior."

"Which she wouldn't have had to do, if he wasn't out of it."

I looked back at the herd, still standing close to junior, nuzzling him, "So because he was out of it, the safety of the entire herd was jeopardized?"

"Exactly."

So altered states in humans jeopardize the safety of the individual, but altered states in horses jeopardize the safety of the herd. No wonder they don't happen, I thought to myself, *because the herd won't allow it.* Unlike people who run *from* an individual who doesn't trust his environment, horses run *to* a horse who doesn't trust his environment. Where people are afraid *of* one who is out for it, horses are afraid *for* them.

Thinking back, I had witnessed this before. However, what I had seen my horses do had prevented the state Junior was in.

In the times I had had a nervous young horse, or even a mare who'd just been weaned from her foal, all of the other horses would become exceptionally interested in this horse. Keeper, my rogue thoroughbred off the track, had had that effect on the herd. From the time he arrived, a nervous ball of energy, he created a stir. Often riding him alongside the three pastures that sat behind the house, the horses inside, young or old, would all come running. It was as if Keeper held more interest for them than any other horse. And the effect was the same at the horse shows. Keeper and I would enter the warmup ring and before long, all of the horses warming up would be just as wound up as he was. But it always the mares, the maternal figures of the herd that attended to him the most. Any time he'd have a fit while being worked, they'd all come running. And yet they wouldn't necessarily do this with the other young horses who could be just as playful. With Keeper it was different, his playfulness seemed to signal something beyond a simple curiosity in them. Keeper had an intensity that the mares noticed. An intensity that, unless attended to, would render him unsafe.

So the horses did what herd animals do -- when Keeper's nervousness escalated, they matched it, becoming equally concerned for him. His tenseness would be responded to with a flurry of concerned neighs. In this way, the herd never allowed Keeper's nervousness to move him to a separate emotional plane, and become disconnected from them the way schizophrenics or autistics can from people. And because of this, Keeper, although at times very angry or fitful, never felt misunderstood as psychiatric patients often do. So, instead of beginning to mistrust the horses around him, my rogue thoroughbred continued to turn to them for reassurance. Because they had responded to his reactions in a way that matched them and offered concern, *he had no reason not to trust them*. However, had my group of horses turned from him as people might have, he most likely would have resorted to an alternative form of coping, such as weaving. But for Keeper, unlike for Junior, was had been artificially separated from the horses around him, the herd had stepped in and prevented it.

Maybe the horses were, for Junior, like the rescue I had provided my client.

Chapter Ten

Imprisoned

"*A*ll of these women have been here before?" I asked, pulling a huge stack of manila file folders out of the dark wooden file cabinet sitting to the left of Tina's desk.

"That's not all. There's those too," she nodded toward a pile of folders on her desk.

I glanced over at her already overloaded desk, stacks of paper, folders, and books mounded on top of one another, completely covering the mouse pad, "You're kidding."

Turning toward me, her soft brown hair framing her face, she sighed, "I wish I were."

She should know. Tina McDowell was regarded in Ventura County as the woman who started women's recovery. Yet at the time, maybe it was her own recovery that she was after. Having just been left by her husband of 18 years, for a younger woman, an exotic lifestyle in Thailand, and escape from a huge tax bill. It was double life, that, years later, she was still unraveling. A corporate lawyer, travel and expense accounts were not outside the norm, Tina never questioned when he said he'd "handled" the taxes. Apparently handling them meant evading them – they hadn't been paid in 11 years – approximately the same amount of time he had been a corporate lawyer. But it wasn't the tax bill that most angered, or even surprised, her – he had always been a private person – it was the fact that the "college fund" he had set up for her three boys, ages 13, 15, and 18, had been absconded with. It, if it ever did exist, would now provide a lavish lifestyle for a lucky young Thai woman. And after years of encouraging her to "stay home and just take care of the boys," Tina was left with no resources. Teaching surfing, which had previously been nothing more than an excuse to exercise her own passion, and live near the beach, now was supposed to support a family of four.

Perhaps it was this forced accounting of her life that made her return to school. Or maybe it was an attempt to make sense of her own grief and anger, but for whatever reason, Tina decided to enter a masters program for marriage, family and child counseling. And somewhere along the way, she became interested in women's recovery.

Mostly she didn't want to leave Ventura California, the small quiet beach town she had called home her entire life, and now her sons' hometown as well. But the closer she came to completing her degree, the more obvious the lack of services for women in Ventura turned out to be. Realizing that it was not just her own desire to work with women such as herself, there was another reason for the abundance of underserved women in the quaint beach town: it was mecca for homelessness. The Ventura river bottom that she had played in as a kid had long been recognized as an underground homeless community. Scattered with tents and sleeping bags, the banks of the river bottom provided shelter form the wind, while the brush offered a place to hide if necessary. And the weather is mild, Ventura is one of the places that outdoor living is quite possible year round. The community, however, had turned a cold shoulder on the infiltration of their town, preferring to deny the problem, and support police programs that discouraged homelessness.

Sitting on the soft burgundy couch that lined the east wall of her office, I opened the first of several files to go over before meeting the women. I had asked to meet with Tina because she had access to the numbers. Of all the trauma based programs nationwide, her programs had seen more people than most other programs combined. Although she specialized in women, creating treatment services for women with children, women expecting children, and women with little more than the clothes on their back – the remnants of a life gone awry – she also created programs for the families of these women, even working with the frequently resistant abusive men. "Look at this," I said, lifting the file closer to my face to make sure I had read the scribbled intake form correctly, "this women was put in jail for 10 days because she failed to tie her dog up as she used the public restroom."

"Keep reading," Tina said without turning from her position bent over a file drawer.

I scrolled down the first page of the woman's file, "My god, her case was delayed three times at the public defender's request."

Tina was still looking through the packed file drawer, "Amazing isn't it?"

"And that's not the first time she's been in either," I flipped the page, "she's had six other infractions – sleeping on a park bench, trespassing, drunk in public, soliciting, arguing with a police officer, and disturbing the peace." I put the file down and picked up the next one, "Are they all like this?"

"See for yourself," Tina handed me a piece of paper she had pulled out of the file drawer.

Taking the paper, I scanned through the rows and columns of abbreviations each with a corresponding number, "What does, TDR stand for?"

Turning her chair from the file drawer, she scooted closer to me, and pulled her glasses off her face, "That's To-Date-Recidivism; it means the percentage of women who return for services."

I looked at the number under the first column, "73% of the women who you saw in 1998, were return customers?"

"That's right," she shifted her athletic frame and sat back in her chair.

Scanning across the row from year to year, I noticed a trend, "These numbers don't go down – 73%, 68%, 75%, 72%, 67% – why are all these women returning?"

She paused, and looked past me for a moment, "That's what happens with trauma."

"But," I paused too, looking around the room as if I had missed something, "these are recidivism rates. Doesn't that just mean that they return for treatment as a court order?" Ventura county, as all other counties in California had been under the guidelines of Proposition 36 which gave all drug related offenders the choice between jail time and treatment services.

"That is *how* the return, but not *why* they return."

I noticed the toys gathered in a basket in the corner of Tina's office. Amongst the disheveled desk and stuffed bookcase, they gave her office a homey feel. "Well then why *do* they return?"

"It's called repetition compulsion," she said, placing her glasses back on.

"Repetition what?"

"Compulsion," she shifted in her chair again, crossing her legs, "It means that they are compelled to repeat the trauma of their past."

"But why?"

She turned and pulled a file off of her desk, "Here, look at this."

I took the file opening it to the intake page, "What am I looking for?"

"Where it begins."

"What begins?" I asked, scrolling down the page.

"Her trauma."

I flipped the first page back to uncover the section that read "Client History." "Abandoned by her mother at age four, went to live with her grandmother, who then rejected her, turning over custody to child services, who then placed her with a foster family, who turned her back over to child services, who placed her again, and she was turned back again, then…"

"Six times."

"Six times she was returned to child services before the age of sixteen, that's unbelievable." I set the file down and looked at Tina, "So what does all this mean?"

Tina glanced at the folder, "Well look at the treatment history."

Picking up the file again, I flipped back to the third page, "She's been kicked out of every program she's been in."

"That's right."

"Why?"

Tina leaned forward in her chair, "Well the *how* is because she brings in drugs, but the *why* is because she is compelled to repeat the abandonment."

I pulled up the pages on the opposite side of the folder. They were filled with case notes from various counselors, interns, psychiatrists, and some from Tina herself, "But why would she be compelled to repeat her abandonment?"

Tina leaned forward in her chair again, and looked over her glasses, "Because on an unconscious level, she believes that she will be rejected."

"Unconsciously?"

She nodded, "Yes, she is not aware that she believes that."

I glanced over at the dark oak bookcase that sat to the left of Tina's desk, teeming full of books with names like *Learned Helplessness, Battered Women,* and, *Left Behind,* it seemed overwhelming, "So when you say she is compelled to repeat her abandonment, she is also not aware, consciously, of that compulsion."

"That's right."

"Then will she always do things to be abandoned?"

Sitting back again, Tina took her glasses off, "Yes, she will sabotage caring relationships, act in ways that force people to reject her, do things like bring drugs into treatment centers – basically put people in positions to almost *have to* abandon her."

I fingered the pages on the left side of the folder, "All because of her initial trauma of being abandoned?"

"Yes," Tina watched as I lifted each page slowly, "she will be confined by her unconscious beliefs."

It was starting to make sense, "And because she is always acting in ways to be abandoned, and then always being abandoned, she will continue to have that belief."

"Exactly," she rotated her glasses between her fingers, "that is what happens with unconscious beliefs – the beliefs themselves, make us live up to them, almost to justify that they are true."

I closed the folder, and set it down again, "In a way so she can say to herself, 'See, I am always being abandoned,'"

Tina nodded again, "All the while, not consciously aware that this is what she is doing."

Looking over at what now seemed like an enormous stack of file folders next to me, and more still on Tina's desk, I asked, "All of these cases have trauma?"

Tina gazed at the stack next to me, "Every one of them."

No surprise the stacks were so large. Trauma causes people to hold unconscious beliefs that make them repeat their trauma. In a way, they remain defined by their trauma.

My eyes still fixed on the stacks, flashes of cases I had worked with ran through my mind. Equine sessions with people battling pervasive trauma are always the most revealing. While traumatized people may have struggled for the majority of their lives, falling in and out of chaos, and never quite feeling "ok," the underlying pathology has usually been quite mystifying. Yet the horses pick up on what is at the root of their turmoil within minutes. A client who had once been referred to me as a complex trauma, with a history of a suspicious plane crash that had never been resolved, and while his family was quite concerned for him, as he had been abusing Effexor and Xanax at increasing rates, they were also confused. Ten years ago, he had boarded a flight leaving Las Vegas and bound for Chicago, that later crashed. My patient was one of only 11 surviving passengers. Yet, mysteriously, there was no record of him ever boarding the flight. While his family certainly didn't want to question his torment, they were concerned about the lack of validity of his story. When he began working with a mare of mine, she immediately began to circle around him closely, tenderly nuzzling his arms and face, in a protective gesture. Then all of the sudden, she retreated from him, and for the remainder of the session kept a distance from him, while my middle aged, single, male client became increasingly angry about the situation. Clear that being doted on by others was his preference, and that my mare was reflecting the lack of need for my client to be cared for, I asked if he occasionally resorts to "alternative measures" to ensure this response in people.

Smiling deceptively, my client nodded. What was later revealed was that he'd actually never been on the flight, and concocted the whole story because, as the youngest child of an alcoholic family, he'd always felt overlooked. And yet, as much as he wanted the attention of those around him, and craved for it, he also had an unconscious need to feel overlooked, just as he had as a child. When his family had questioned him about the crash, and what he was experiencing as a result, his vague responses had effectively prevented them from providing what he so wanted. They simply didn't know what to do. My client's story, despite being designed to elicit care, did just the opposite. As he was unable to answer their questions directly and harboring an exaggerated lie, he only felt more separate from them, and they felt more confused by him. This story, along with my client's aloof behavior, had gone on for years, as had his prescription drug abuse. Yet what had never been made clear was his unconscious need to recreate the childhood that originally traumatized him.

These very unconscious needs are exactly what horses respond to. While on a conscious level, a person may think she needs one thing or another, but to a horse, the greater necessity is what is not conscious, and therefore, not being expressed. As these unexpressed -- unconscious -- motives disrupt communication, to a herd animal, who depends on implicit communication to determine safety, resolving what is unconscious always takes precedence. And resolving what is unconscious means forcing the expression of feelings that exist within the person, yet are in one way or another, to overwhelming to be expressed. So a horse may do just as my mare had, responding to my client's need to be abandoned. What she was actually trying to get him to do was resolve this feeling by approaching her and initiating contact. To her, a herd animal, his unconscious need to be abandoned will jeopardize his safety, as a herd animal depends on the existence of a group to fend off predators. Her withdrawal from my client was her only way of trying to get him to avoid the need to be abandoned, and do what he needed to do to be safe -- which is reach out for contact. While my client "wanted" my mare to be close to him, he "needed" her to move away so that he may resolve his need to be left alone. And his family had, for years, attempted to give my client what he wanted, all the while unaware of what was occurring unconsciously with him.

Handing the massive stack of case notes back to Tina, I asked, "So if people keep acting on their unconscious beliefs, and others continue to respond to these beliefs, making them true, can people really help each other ever break free of their trauma?"

Tina looked at me curiously, "Only those who recognize it."

"Who are those?"

"Well," She paused, tilting her head to the side, "mostly therapists."

Watching the hands of the clock tick slowly on the wall behind Tina, memories of the first ride on Nimo flashed through my mind, "And maybe horses," I whispered.

Head still tilted to the side, Tina looked a bit perplexed.

Chapter Eleven

Mary, John, And Kate

*A*s I shifted my weight and rested my chin on rail of the fence, the rays of light just beginning to emerge through the thick fog gave the small arena a celestial glow. The branches of old oak tree that stood near the middle of the arena reached out across the arena like arms offering solace. It was quiet this morning, and only the rustling of an occasional chipmunk in the brush broke the silence. The moisture from the early morning fog had collected on the leaves of the oak tree and the air smelled fresh like dew on freshly cut grass.

I had been watching Nimo quietly standing next to Mary as she shifted around unsure why he wasn't moving. A patient at the treatment center I had just begun contracting with, she had only met Nimo a few weeks before. But from the very first meeting, Nimo had taken a keen interest in her.

"What is he doing?" she asked as Nimo moved closer to her, nudging her intently. Nudging is something Nimo did when he wanted to bring life to someone. In the same way I had seen mares do this with young foals when they want them to stand, it was a way to convey a sense that someone is lacking vitality, or weak in some way. They will especially do this if a sick one lays down, disrupting the natural vitality of the herd. Being herd animals, their safety depends on maintaining continuity, I knew this. But it isn't just continuity in presence, it 's emotional continuity. It's their instinct. They can't help it, when one horse becomes anxious, they all become anxious. It should be the same with people, but people often hide their emotions. I did, it's part of responding to trauma. But people's bodies still register the emotions. Mary wasn't the first person Nimo had noticed this with. Watching many of the patients that came from the treatment center, they looked okay on the outside, but Nimo would not stop nudging them. He'd be insistent about it, too, as if to say, they may look fine, but they are not ok.

A few of the patients, like John, a young college student who had been intervened on by his parents for an amphetamine addiction, became angry with Nimo when he did this. With John, Nimo had been nudging, yes, but he had also been herding him. Circling around him repeatedly with his head held high and posture elevated, he seemed to be saying something more than 'John is not safe.' It was as if he was trying to provoke him, almost encouraging him to be angry. It wasn't until John actually became angry, threw his arms up, and yelled, "Stop it," at Nimo, that he stopped. The anger that John expressed was not actually meant for Nimo, but was an expression of the anger he felt at his parent's invasive control and foregone expectation that he would go to medical school. Yet he couldn't express it, for fear that they would reject him, and remove financial support. He didn't want to go to medical school, and his amphetamine addiction was his only way to say so. Nimo had been right, John was unsafe. But he was unsafe because he could not express his anger. Nimo's provoking of it was the only way he could bring what was tormenting John to the surface. And after, John did feel much more safe. With the support of the treatment center, he finally was bale to communicate his wishes to his parents.

Looking back at Nimo, standing right next to Mary, almost leaning toward her, I thought back to the first time I rode him. Mary, like many patients, had wanted to ride Nimo too. When Mary had asked, I thought about the way her relationships had been. Almost selfishly, she had always wanted more than the other person could give. But I also understood her desire to just be free, the way being on the back of a horse makes you feel. I had been there too, thrown caution out the window, just to feel free. Just as it had been irresponsible of me to ride Nimo the first time with no helmet, no lungeing, and no one else around in case I got hurt, it would have been irresponsible of me to put Mary on Nimo when she asked. And actually she was asking the wrong person. The decision was not up to me, it was up to Nimo – just like when I rode him for the first time.

And while I knew I was acting desperately that day, I had no idea how trapped and scared I actually felt. But he did. "He doesn't want to leave you." I answered, as Nimo nibbled at Mary's belt buckle, unfazed with her uneasiness.

"Why?' she asked

"You are not safe alone." I answered, as Mary looked at me perplexed, and Nimo circled around her repeatedly. Different from the circling he had done with John, Nimo's posture was lowered, his head was held low, and his body was curved around Mary. With John he had almost seemed to be trying to push him over, or move him around. What I was watching Nimo do with Mary was herding, but it was the same thing I had often watched mares do with their foals. It is also what the herd does with a weak or injured horse. A way to shield the injured or weak one from anything threatening, the herd will position themselves around them in a circle. If it is just one horse, like with a mare and foal, the mare has to keep moving around the circle to keep all sides protected. This is exactly what Nimo was doing with Mary.

"Why is he doing that? It makes me nervous" she held her arms up in front of her as if to defend herself.

"He is protecting you, and you feel as though you need to defend yourself," I answered. A common response to trauma, many patients had also learned to mistrust protection. Another patient, Kate, who was 38, had grown up with a schizophrenic mother, and been a victim of sexual abuse at the age of 13, had also learned not to trust protection. For her, like Mary, what should have been protection simply wasn't safe. Instead, her mother's erratic behavior, and her father's frequent absences left Kate to fend for herself. Instead of being cared for, she channeled her energy into caring for her younger brother. For her, the feeling of protection Nimo was trying to offer actually felt threatening. Then Nimo would move away, respecting her fear. But then she'd feel lonely. Nimo's protection and subsequent withdrawal was his only way to invoke the loneliness Kate had kept hidden from the world. It was this loneliness that had made her unsafe, and she had actually brought herself to the treatment center after two serious bouts of clinical depression. She had struggled on for weeks, managing her demanding job as an accountant, and staying late at work to avoid returning to an empty house, before she finally collapsed and couldn't make herself get out of bed anymore. Working with Nimo for four weeks, she had been caught in a bind. She wanted to feel safe, and didn't want Nimo to leave, yet, she felt threatened when he circled her. In the same way she found herself caring for people, yet avoiding letting herself be cared for, Nimo's circling and withdrawal was his only way of saying "Your discomfort with being cared for is making you lonely." It was also his way of conveying that for Kate to feel safe, her relationships had to always feel as if they were in her control. The comfort Nimo was trying to offer was simply not in Kate's control, and it wasn't until she finally let go, and accepted the direction of the treatment center that she realized that her job, her life, and everything in it, were all ways for her to feel in control, have people depend on her, and avoid depending on anyone else. She did finally quit her job, moved to California and began studying psychology.

Mary shared with Kate, the feeling that protection people should have given her had never felt safe. She had grown up the child of immigrant parents from Spain, who transplanted themselves in New York, while her mother attempted to rekindle her dreams of becoming a movie star through Mary. While Mary struggled with being a six year child in a foreign country and nothing, or nobody, familiar, her mother primped, posed her and dragged her to every modeling and casting audition she could find. Vehement in her control, her mother would also go through periods of uncontrollable rage, often throwing things and shouting wildly. The fights between her parents would always end with her father leaving, sometimes for a few hours, and more often, for a few days. Finally, he came home one day and announced that the family must move back to Spain. Mary later learned that her father had been implicated by the Securities and Exchange Commission in a ring of corruption. Leaving was the only way to avoid going to jail.

Once back in Spain, her father's periods of absence continued, while her mother's drinking escalated. Her older brother, Ryan, four years her senior, was now fourteen, and without any father figure, or male role model. Uprooted from his friends not once, but twice, and ignored totally by his mother, he became rageful at Mary. Sneaking into her room at night, he would torture her, physically, and then sexually. When she would try to scream for help, he would threaten her, and tape her mouth shut. The abuse continued, unnoticed, for three years.

However, Mary's roles began to land her some acclaim, and her mother began sending Mary's face sheet and biography to agents in New York. In a fortuitous turn, Mary was cast in a movie with legendary actor, who took a special interest in her, noticing her potential. Working with him stirred Mary's love of acting, and she was adored by the cast and crew as "a natural". The reviews were effusive with praise, and her fame exploded. With her fame, however, also came the public scrutiny, and she was called "worst dressed," "fat," and then, "anorexic". Mary had never been fat, yet any off angle shot that might reveal a less than perfect body was fuel for the vicious paparazzi.

The pressure to maintain the perfect body constant, Mary soon turned to drugs. What had started as a "few pills to make it through the day" soon became a daily ritual. Mary found herself horribly addicted as her diet soon consisted of nothing more than cigarettes, coffee, and crack, affectionately known as the "three C's" diet in the industry. She soon became dangerously thin, days blurred together, and her muscles deteriorated as her body struggled to function. Simple tasks like standing became difficult, and it soon became more comfortable to be unconscious. Finally, an overdose and an emergency room visit revealed fluid in her lungs and little chance of recovery. For all intents and purposes, many had written Mary off as dead.

Many times she had wanted to die. While she loved the acting, it was also the vehicle of what had been the exploitation of her entire life. She had learned that the only safety she found in the world was through avoiding it.

"He's not moving" Mary noticed. It was her fifth time working with Nimo. "Why is he not moving?" she asked.

"It appears as though you no longer need him too," I answered, thinking back to the last several visits where Nimo had relentlessly nudged and circled Mary. Each time she became overwhelmed, he would move away a little, noticing her mistrust his protection. Then she would begin to feel alone, and he would return. Like Kate, as Mary had vacillated between feeling threatened by Nimo's protection, and not wanting to be alone, he had moved from circling her to keeping a distance from her. He was respecting both her need for protection, and her fear of it. It was his way of saying that it was up to her to resolve the conflict she felt.

This pattern had continued for the past four weeks, but Mary had also begun to find some solace in her life. She had returned to stage acting and had been cast in a few plays, including a well acclaimed one in New York. Avoiding public scrutiny, she was able to pursue her love in a way that didn't expose her. She had also reconnected with her grandmother, who had for years, she later discovered, tried to contact her, and been discouraged by her mother. With the support of the friends she had made in recovery, her grandmother, and her love of acting rekindled, Mary had finally begun to feel as if she wanted to live.

"What does that mean?" she asked as she turned toward Nimo inquisitively. He arched his neck and raised his head as he noticed something stirring in the brush just outside the fence. He took a few steps toward it, then stopped and looked back at Mary. She noticed it too, and noticed that Nimo wasn't returning back to her.

"It means you are free."

Although Mary had forgotten that she actually wanted to ride Nimo, I would have let her if she asked.

Recommended Reading

1. *The Soul of a Horse: Life Lessons from the Herd, by Joe Camp*

   (Random House/Harmony Books, 2008).

   ISBN-10: 0307406865

   ISBN-13: 978-0307406866

   If you liked the sort of connection is examined in ON THE BACK OF A HORSE, and the search for *how* horses understand people better than they often understand themselves, you will most likely enjoy Joe Camp's bestselling story of his introduction to horses, and how he learned just what it means to be a herd animal.

2. *The Tao of Equus: A Woman's Journey of Healing and Transformation through the Way of the Horse, by Linda Kohanov*

   (New World Library, 2007).

   ISBN-10: 1577314204

   ISBN-13: 978-1577314202

   Like ON THE BACK OF A HORSE, Linda Kohanov's bestseller examines the relationship between a woman and a horse. If you enjoyed the almost spiritual connection between humans and horses explored in ON THE BACK OF A HORSE, you will most definitely be fascinated by the emotional growth and healing experienced in *The Tao of Equus*.

3, The Man Who Listens to Horses: The Story of a Real life horse Whisperer, by Monty Roberts

(Random House, 1997).

ISBN-10: 0345510453

ISBN-13: 978-0345510457

If you enjoyed the story of how horses heal people told in ON THE BACK OF A HORSE, you will absolutely want to read Monty Roberts bestselling account of just how he came to understand horses innately as he does. As Roberts tells the story of a childhood rife with trauma, he also explains clearly and comprehensively the amazing equine language that fascinates us all.

4. The Horse Boy: A Father's Quest to Heal His Son , by Rupert Isaacson

(Little Brown and Company, 2009).

ISBN-10: 0316008230

ISBN-13: 978-0316008235

The Horse Boy offers a rare insight into the ways autism can disrupt the ability to connect with the world and the people in it, and a parent's desire for understanding and healing. Like ON THE BACK OF A HORSE, this fascinating book examines how time-honored equine principles can heal those struggling with the trauma of mental illness.

5. Horses with a Mission: Extraordinary True Stories of Equine Service by Allen Anderson and Linda Allen

(New World Library, 2009)

ISBN-10: 1577316487

ISBN-13: 978-1577316480

If you liked the study of equine instinct and healing in ON THE BACK OF A HORSE, you will also enjoy the dramatic stories of just what can happen when horses and humans are allowed to follow these instincts told by authors Allen and Anderson.

6. Hope Rising: Stories from the Ranch of Rescued Dreams by Kim Meeder

(Multnomah Books, 2003)

ISBN-10: 1590522699

ISBN-13: 978-1590522691

Hope Rising is a story of inspiration as Meeder describes numerous accounts of horses reaching children where people have failed. If the case histories and examples offered in ON THE BACK OF A HORSE, interested you, you will certainly enjoy this both heart-wrenching and uplifting book.

7. Chosen By a Horse, by Susan Richards

(Soho Press, 2007)

ASIN: B000SMQFWW

Not so much an understanding of equine language and healing, as is ON THE BACK OF A HORSE, *Chosen By a Horse* offers a powerful story of equine inspiration and hope. If you liked the narrative style and real life examples shared in ON THE BACK OF A HORSE, you will most definitely enjoy Richard's book.

8. Learning Their Language: Intuitive Communication with Animals and Nature by Marta

Williams and D.V.M. Cheryl Schwartz

(New World Library, 2003)

ISBN-10: 1577312430

ISBN-13: 978-1577312437

Told by animal communicator Marta Williams, this book describes the basis of animal communication, and gives you a step by step guide to learning how to communicate with animals. Like ON THE BACK OF A HORSE, Williams provides a scientific, well founded, approach to learning animal language interspersed with real life stories of people who speak to animals.

Author Biography

Claire Dorotik's specialization is equine-facilitated psychotherapy. Her approach has been utilized by many recovery centers, including Creative Care Recovery and The Canyon Recovery Center. She has written many articles for *Horsetrader, Ride,* and *Flying Changes* magazines and is a contributor to *Equine Therapy: Straight Talk From The Horse's Mouth,* a course for psychotherapists, currently offered by the Zur Institute in San Diego. She lives in Colorado with her two horses Kona and Admiral.